MONTEREY PENINSULA

AND SANTA CRUZ

HOW TO USE THIS GUIDEBOOK

This guidebook is divided into four sections: *An Introduction to the Monterey Peninsula, The History of the Monterey Peninsula, The Monterey Peninsula,* and *Santa Cruz.*

The first two sections comprise essays designed to provide you with facts on the area.

In the next two sections, we explore the Monterey Peninsula and Santa Cruz region, with a detailed geographical breakdown of the area. Each section contains descriptions of the various places and points of interest, followed by a subsection entitled *Practical Information.* The *Practical Information* is designed to provide you with a ready reference to accommodations, restaurants, places of interest, seasonal events, recreation, tours, etc., with hours, prices, addresses and phone numbers.

A quick and easy way into this book is the *Index* at the end.

California Series

The Complete Gold Country Guidebook
The Complete Lake Tahoe Guidebook
The Complete Monterey Peninsula Guidebook
The Complete San Diego Guidebook
The Complete San Francisco Guidebook
The Complete Wine Country Guidebook
Vacation Towns of California

Hawaii Series

The Complete Kauai Guidebook
The Complete Maui Guidebook
The Complete Oahu Guidebook
The Complete Big Island of Hawaii Guidebook

Mexico Series

The Complete Baja California Guidebook
The Complete Yucatan Peninsula Guidebook

Indian Chief Travel Guides are available from your local bookstore or Indian Chief Publishing House, P.O. Box 5205, Tahoe City, CA 96145.

The Complete
MONTEREY
PENINSULA
AND SANTA CRUZ
Guidebook

Published by Indian Chief Publishing House
Tahoe City, California

Area Editor: **B. SANGWAN**
Editorial Associate: **PHILLIPPA J. SAVAGE**
Photographs: **Lee Foster, B. Sangwan,
 Monterey Peninsula Chamber of Commerce,
 Santa Cruz Boardwalk, Big Trees Railroad**

ISBN 0-916841-32-4

CONTENTS

Map of the Monterey Peninsula   6

AN INTRODUCTION TO THE MONTEREY PENINSULA —   7
  "The Greatest Meeting of Land and Water in the World"

THE HISTORY OF THE MONTEREY PENINSULA —   9
  California's First Capital

THE MONTEREY PENINSULA — History, Golf and Steinbeck   15
Map of Monterey   18-19
Map of Cannery Row   24
Map of Pacific Grove   28-29
Map of Pebble Beach   32-33
Map of Carmel-by-the-Sea   36-37
Map of Carmel Valley   40
Map of Point Lobos Reserve State Park   43
Map of Big Sur   46-47

Practical Information   54
Map of Monterey Path of History   78-79

SANTA CRUZ — "Surf City, USA"   99
Map of Santa Cruz   102-103
Map of San Lorenzo Valley   105
Map of Capitola-Soquel-Aptos   107

Practical Information   110

INDEX   139

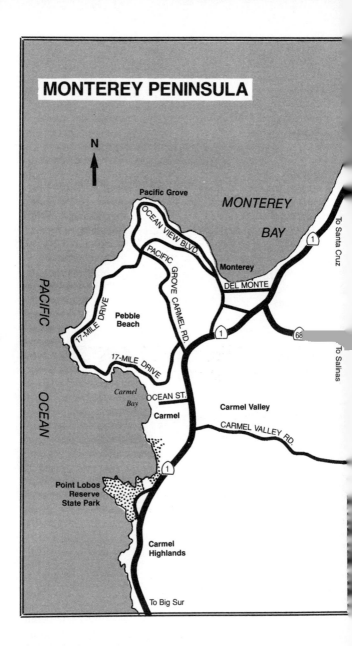

MONTEREY PENINSULA

N

Pacific Grove

MONTEREY

BAY

OCEAN VIEW BLVD.

PACIFIC GROVE CARMEL RD.

Monterey

DEL MONTE

To Santa Cruz

1

PACIFIC

17-MILE DRIVE

Pebble Beach

17-MILE DRIVE

1

68

To Salinas

OCEAN

Carmel Bay

OCEAN ST.

Carmel

Carmel Valley

CARMEL VALLEY RD.

1

Point Lobos Reserve State Park

Carmel Highlands

To Big Sur

AN INTRODUCTION TO THE MONTEREY PENINSULA

"The Greatest Meeting of Land and Water in the World"

The Monterey Peninsula is breathtakingly scenic, with its white-foam cypress-lined coastline, its picture-perfect aquamarine bay, and dramatic cliffs overhanging famous Big Sur. Indeed, Robert Louis Stevenson once described it as "the greatest meeting of land and water in the world."

The Monterey Peninsula comprises approximately 35 square miles of coastal wilderness, situated along the north Central Coast of California, some 125 miles south of San Francisco (345 miles from Los Angeles). To its north lies Monterey Bay, to its west the Pacific Ocean, and to the south, Big Sur, offering in it one of the world's most spectacular coastal drives. The peninsula itself is made up of white-sand beaches and craggy cliffs, cypress forests and low, coastal hills, sea lion colonies, ocean-front greens and fairways, sand dunes, and fertile valleys fanning out farther inland. There is also on the peninsula the historic city of Monterey, California's first capital and one of its oldest settlements, and the delightful little towns of Pacific Grove and Carmel-by-the-Sea, tourist meccas, no less.

The Monterey Peninsula attracts nearly 3 million tourists

each year, and an additional 2 million or so visit the nearby beach city of Santa Cruz, just to the north, mostly during the summer months. There are over 6000 hotel rooms in the Monterey area alone, and more than 300 restaurants in the Monterey Peninsula and Santa Cruz areas. There are also well over 200 art galleries here, and an abundance of recreational facilities, including whale-watching (in season), fishing, riding, tennis, gallery-browsing, antique hunting, boat cruises, and — best of all — golf, with no fewer than 20 superb, championship golf courses, among them the world-renowned Pebble Beach Golf Links and the Cypress Point, Spyglass Hill and Del Monte courses And to add to this, the Monterey Peninsula enjoys a delightful, temperate climate, with temperatures ranging from 60° in summer to around 50° in winter.

Indeed, the Monterey Peninsula — together with the Santa Cruz area — is one of California's foremost tourist regions, at once historic and scenic.

THE HISTORY OF THE MONTEREY PENINSULA

California's First Capital

The earliest known inhabitants of the Monterey Peninsula were the Esselen, a Hokan-speaking, primordial people who inhabited the area for nearly 2,500 years, from around 1500 B.C. to more or less 500 A.D. Between 500 B.C. and 500 A.D., the Ohlone Indians displaced the Esselen along much of the north-central coast of California, extending their range from Monterey Bay north to San Francisco Bay. The Ohlone lived in some 40 different tribes. In the Monterey area, their main village was known as Rumsen — situated on the south side of the Carmel River — and the Ohlone inhabiting Rumsen and the surrounding areas, in turn, also came to be known as the Rumsen. (The Spanish, however, later referred to them as the *Costanoans*, derived from *Costanos*, a Spanish term for "coastal people.")

In 1542, Juan Rodriguez Cabrillo, a Portugese sailor, sailing for Spain, discovered Monterey Bay while exploring the coast of California. He claimed the entire coast of California for Spain. Sixty years later, in 1602, Sebastian Vizcaino, a Spanish explorer, sailed into Monterey Bay and landed on its south shore, at the site of present-day Monterey. He, too, claimed the entire coast of California for the King of Spain, and named the bay

"Monterey," for his patron, the Count of Monte Rey, viceroy of New Spain.

Monterey, however, was not settled until 1770. In June of that year, Captain Gaspar de Portola, Governor of Baja California, and Father Junipero Serra, a Franciscan missionary, founded the town of Monterey, at the very same site where Sebastian Vizcaino had landed in 1602. Portola built here, that same year, the first of California's four Spanish presidios. The presidio was located directly above the site of Vizcaino's landing, on Presidio Hill; it comprised a small, crude fortification, El Castillo, and a handful of smaller, adobe and thatch dwellings. Father Serra, meanwhile, established here, also that same year, Mission San Carlos de Borromeo, the second of California's 21 Franciscan missions, which, a year later, in 1771, he moved to its present site in Carmel, overlooking the Carmel River.

During the next two decades, new settlements were created in the Monterey region, a code of laws known as the Reglamento was instituted, and Monterey was firmly established as the Spanish capital of California. In the 1790s and early 1800s, too, representatives from several different countries visited Monterey, as well as other parts of California. Notable among them were George Vancouver, a British commissioner who arrived here on a tour of the Pacific coast in 1792, and French nobleman Compte de La Perouse, representing the French government. Both Vancouver and La Perouse noted that California "cried out for development," but that under Spanish rule this was not likely to occur.

In 1821, Mexico won its independence from Spain, and a year later, in the spring of 1822, news of Mexico's independence reached California. In Monterey, the flag of the Republic of Mexico quickly replaced that of Spain, and on November 9, 1822, under Mexican rule, the first California legislature convened here, with representatives from throughout the proposed state. Several radical democratic reforms were enacted, foremost among them a new constitution guaranteeing every citizen in Mexico — and in the territory of California — the right to vote — and this at a time when in the United States of America such ethnic minorities as Indians and Black Americans were denied a vote!

The end of Spanish rule in California also brought to prominence a new group of people — the *Californios*. The *Californios*, typically, were the offspring of Spanish settlers, who had been born and raised in California. They included such prominent figures as Mariano Guadalupe Vallejo, Juan Bautista Alvarado and Jose Castro, among others. These men, most of them young, liberal, and with new ideas, became the political leaders of California. They secularized the Spanish missions, and awarded some of the earliest land grants, mostly to family and friends, creating a new, privileged class of native-born *Californios*. They were also instrumental in introducing in California free trade, which, under Spanish rule, had been outlawed. Trade, much of it in California cattle hides, flourished along the coast of California, including the Monterey Peninsula, and brought to the region prosperity. Among the earliest and most successful traders in the area were William Hartnell and Hugh McCulloch, two Britishers, and John R. Cooper, half brother to Thomas Oliver Larkin, the first U.S. Consul to California.

The late 1820s and early 1830s also ushered in a period of growth in the region. The town of Monterey, in fact, began to spread beyond the old Presidio, with scores of new dwellings — largely single-story adobe structures — scattering along the broad, green shelf of land above the bay. In 1835, American writer Richard Henry Dana, when visiting Monterey, made note of the new dwellings in the developing town, describing Monterey in his book, *Two Years Before The Mast*, as "the pleasantest and most civilized-looking place in California." In 1835, also, Thomas Larkin, who had arrived in Monterey in 1832, built here a splendid, two-story home, with adobe walls and wooden balconies, combining both the Spanish and New England styles of architecture. The Larkin House became the model for a new, unique Monterey-Colonial style of architecture, and in the following years several new structures were built in the "Monterey" style, notable among them the Pacific House, Casa Soberanes and Casa Alvarado.

The year 1846 brought war to California. After an attempt by the United States to purchase the territory of California from Mexico failed, and following, immediately, the Bear Flag Revolt — an American-led uprising — in Sonoma, farther to the north of Monterey, war erupted between the two nations. And in July, 1846, Commodore John Drake Sloat, under direct orders from Washington to occupy the port of Monterey in the event of war between Mexico and the United States, sailed into Monterey Bay aboard his flagship, the *Savannah*, and landed at the Monterey wharf an American contingent of 140 sailors and 85 marines under the command of Captain William Mervine. The Americans raised the American flag at the Custom House, and claimed Monterey and, indeed, the entire territory of California for the United States. This, effectively, ended Mexican rule in California.

Monterey's early American period, however, was remarkably brief. In 1846, Walter Colton, who had arrived in Monterey as the U.S. naval chaplain on board the *Congress*, under Sloat's command, became the first American alcalde (chief magistrate and mayor) of Monterey. He built in the center of the city, that same year, the elegant Colton Hall, one of the most distinguished buildings of the early American period, and also published here, in 1846, California's first newspaper, the *Californian*, printed in both English and Spanish. A few years later, in 1849, Monterey became the site of California's first Constitutional Convention, and 48 delegates from throughout the proposed State of California gathered at Colton Hall to draft, debate and ratify a constitution for the State of California. It was an historic event, and Monterey's greatest hour. Ironically, however, this also signaled the end of Monterey's days of glory: the capital of California then shifted northward, by popular vote, to San Jose, San Francisco, and, finally, Sacramento.

In the following years, Monterey declined in status and importance, politically, socially and economically. In fact, by 1859, the city of Monterey was so bankrupt that the city council was forced to sell all the lands belonging to the town — totalling some 30,000 acres — for a meager $1,002.50. And by 1869, Monterey's resident population had dwindled to fewer than 400, and the San Jose *Mercury* reported, "one third of the buildings of Monterey appear vacant. The lazy vultures roost upon the roofs and cock their eyes at all newcomers with a sort of regretful expression, as if to say, 'Please don't disturb us.'"

During the late 1800s, however, the peace and quiet and beauty of the Monterey Peninsula began attracting to the region poets, writers and artists, foremost among them Scottish-born writer Robert Louis Stevenson, who arrived here in 1879, and who, standing on the Monterey coast, observed, "on no other coast that I know shall you enjoy, in calm, sunny weather, such a spectacle of Ocean's greatness, such beauty of changing color, or such degrees of thunder in the sound." Another, poet Charles Warren Stoddard wrote of Monterey's fabulous Del Monte Forest: "Blood-red sunsets flood this haunted wood. The moonlight fills it with mystery; and along its rocky front, where the sea flowers blossom and the sea-grass waves its glossy locks, the soul of the poet and artist meet and mingle between shadowless sea and cloudless sky, in the unsearchable mystery of that cypress solitude."

In the late 1800s and early 1900s, also, the Monterey Peninsula spawned a new industry: tourism. In 1875, Pacific Grove, adjoining to the west of Old Monterey, was founded as a "Christian Seaside resort"; in January, 1880, the Southern Pacific Railroad arrived in Monterey; and in June, 1880, the Hotel Del Monte, located at the neck of the Monterey Peninsula and hailed as the "Saratoga of the Pacific," opened to the public, offering, among other amenities, a racecourse, a polo field, a swimming pool, and running hot and cold water and a telephone in every room! Vacationers and socialites from San Francisco began arriving in Monterey by the thousands, both by car and on board Southern Pacific's "Del Monte Express"; and in 1919, the newly-formed Del Monte Properties Company — headed by

Samuel Morse, grand-nephew of the inventor of the telegraph — purchased nearly 8,000 acres of land on the Monterey Peninsula, encompassing the virgin Del Monte Forest and the oceanfront tract now known as Pebble Beach, and built at the southern edge of the property The Lodge at Pebble Beach, another luxury resort, which lured such celebrities and personages of the day as Clark Gable, W.C. Fields, Salvador Dali, and, later on, even the John F. Kennedy family. At the turn of the century, too, the Carmel Development Company began developing "Carmel City" — present-day Carmel-by-the-Sea — at the head of Carmel Bay, just south of the peninsula, as an artists' and writers' colony; and by the 1920s, in neighboring Carmel Valley, subdivided, wooded lots were being sold to visitors to the area for the construction of weekend cabins and vacation homes.

Meanwhile, in Monterey, the "Old Pacific Capital," there was yet another industry developing — fishing and canning sardines. In 1900, Frank Booth, a cannery operator from the Sacramento River area, built a small fish-packing plant near Monterey's Fisherman's Wharf, and began fishing and canning sardines, which he found to be plentiful in the Monterey Bay. In 1902, Knute Hovden, a young Norwegian, and a graduate from the National Fisheries College in Norway, arrived upon the scene. Hovden quickly introduced new and more efficient techniques for both fishing and canning the small, silver-sided fish, with purse-bottomed brails and impound pens, and — an invention of its day — a machine solderer. A few years later, Pietro Ferrante, a Sicilian immigrant, also moved to Monterey, bringing to the area, over the next few years, several more Sicilian and Italian fishermen, who formed the backbone of Monterey's fishing industry. And the sardine business then grew quickly — by 1913, there were four full-fledged canneries operating along Monterey's waterfront, processing some 25 tons of fish daily; by 1918, the number of canneries located along what by then had come to be known as "Cannery Row," swelled to 27, processing more than 4 million cases of sardines in the course of a year; and by the early 1940s, when Monterey's sardine industry finally peaked and Monterey gained notoriety as the "Sardine Capital of the World," there were over 4,000 workers on the industry payroll, with nearly 250,000 tons of the silver-sided fish being processed each year. But, only a few years later, in 1945, just as surprisingly as the sardines had first appeared in Monterey Bay, they mysteriously disappeared from the bay, bringing to a grinding halt Monterey's multi-million-dollar industry.

In the early 1940s, too, novelist John Steinbeck, who had been born and raised in nearby Salinas, arrived in Monterey, at Cannery Row. Steinbeck wrote of the row — and its cast of characters, which included the bawdy fishermen and cannery workers and eccentrics of sorts—with a passion, immortalizing it in his classics, *Cannery Row* and *Sweet Thursday*. Wrote he of the row: "Cannery Row in Monterey in California is a poem, a stink, a grating noise, a quality of light, a tone, a habit, a nostalgia, a dream. Cannery Row is the gathered and scattered tin and iron and rust and splintered wood, chipped pavement and weedy lots and junk heaps, sardine canneries of corrugated iron, honky tonks, restaurants and whore houses, and little crowded groceries and flop-houses".

The mid and late 1900s, however, in the Monterey Peninsula, have largely been a period of preservation. In Pebble Beach, for instance, the Pebble Beach Company — formerly the Del Monte Properties Company — has preserved much of the Del Monte Forest as a greenbelt, and set aside most oceanfront tracts exclusively for the development of golf courses. In Carmel, a 1916 ordinance, banning the cutting of trees within the town limits, has created in its wake a lush, unrestrained urban forest, adding immensely to the charm and character of the little seaside village. In Pacific Grove, dozens of Victorians in the center of town and along the waterfront have been painstakingly restored, many of them converted into delightful old bed and breakfast establishments. Along the Big Sur coast, substantial acreages and former ranches have been acquired by the California State Parks Department, and preserved as state parks or protected wilderness areas. And in Monterey, the highly active Monterey History and Art Association, originally founded in 1931, has — working closely with the Monterey City Council and the Urban Renewal Agency of Monterey — rescued, restored and preserved scores of old adobes and other historic buildings, and mapped Monterey's famed "Path of History."

Today, the Monterey Peninsula, as a result of its historical and natural preservation, is one of California's loveliest and most historic regions, and its foremost tourist destination.

THE MONTEREY PENINSULA

History, Golf, and Steinbeck

The Monterey Peninsula is one of California's loveliest and most historic regions, located along the north Central Coast of California, directly below Monterey Bay. It has in it thousands of acres of unspoiled coastal wilderness, one or two spectacular nature reserves, with sea-lion colonies and shorebird habitats, and one of California's oldest Spanish settlements, where much still remains from California's past.

The Monterey Peninsula comprises roughly 35 square miles, largely made up of the Del Monte Forest, a fabulous, 8,400-acre cypress forest, which also has in it the world-renowned Pebble Beach, famous as the home of golf. At the north end of the peninsula, along Monterey Bay, are the historic towns of Monterey — the "Old Spanish Capital," founded in 1770 — and Pacific Grove, situated adjacent to one another, with Pacific Grove lying to the west of Monterey; and at the southern end, at the head of Carmel Bay, sits the picturesque little village of Carmel-by-the-Sea. Inland from Carmel and the Del Monte Forest, of course, lies Carmel Valley, much of it still rural, and farther still, eastward, is the fertile Salinas Valley, birthplace of John Steinbeck. And to the south of the Monterey Peninsula itself, stretching some 90 miles along the coastal Santa Lucia mountains, is famous Big Sur, offering in it one of the world's most scenic coastal drives.

The Monterey Peninsula lies approximately 125 miles south of San Francisco (345 miles from Los Angeles), reached more or less directly on the coastal Highway 1. An alternative route is by way of Highway 101 south to Salinas, some 110 miles, then Route 68 southwestward another 15 miles or so to the Monterey Peninsula. There is also a commercial airport on the peninsula, at Monterey, located just to the east of town.

MONTEREY

Clearly, the best starting point for a tour of the Monterey Peninsula is Monterey itself, situated at the top end of the peninsula, along the southern edge of Monterey Bay. It is one of the largest and most important towns on the peninsula, and a good center for visitors to the area, with excellent accommodations and restaurants, art galleries, boutiques, import and specialty shops, and an abundance of recreational facilities, including more than a dozen superb, championship golf courses located quite close to town. Monterey also, we might add, is one of California's most historic towns, originally settled in 1770, and which has been the capital of California under three different banners — Spanish (1770-1822), Mexican (1822-1846) and American (1846-1848) — with its history representing, to a great extent, the history of pre-Gold Rush California.

For the purposes of touring, of course, Monterey can be divided into three primary areas of interest: Old Monterey — which comprises much of the center of town — and Fisherman's Wharf; Cannery Row, of John Steinbeck fame, adjoining directly to the west of Old Monterey; and the nearby communities of Seaside, Sand City, Del Rey Oaks, Fort Ord and Marina, all lying to the east and northeast of Monterey, mostly nestled along the bay, and with a handful of tourist attractions, one or two scenic vistas, and some recreational possibilities.

Old Monterey and Fisherman's Wharf

For history buffs, Monterey is indeed *the* place to visit. It has in it, in the old part of town, no fewer than forty most historic buildings — largely old adobes — dotted along its famed "path of history" in the Monterey State Historic Park, most of them rescued, restored and preserved through the efforts of the highly active Monterey History and Art Association. Most of these can be visited on a self-guided tour, either by walking round or driving, with good maps to go by. A fair number of these contain original 18th- and 19th-century furnishings and artifacts, and delightful, well-kept gardens; while some are still in use, as city or park offices. The State Parks Department, by the way, also has guided tours of many of these old relics, available for a fee of around $1.00 each.

In any event, at the top of the tour is the Custom House Plaza, located at the north end of town, near the waterfront. The plaza itself is quite lovely, brick-paved, and with shade trees, a fountain and *bocce* courts; and it has on it, as its chief attraction, the venerable old Custom House, a splendid, two-story Monterey-

The Lone Cypress Tree, Monterey Peninsula's most famous
landmark, is located on the 17-Mile Drive

The "kelp forest," Monterey Bay Aquarium's largest exhibit, rises three stories

style adobe, with a second-floor balcony overlooking the bay.
The Custom House was originally built in 1814, functioning as
a toll house during the Mexican era, and is claimed to be the
oldest government building on the West Coast. It is also, equally
importantly, the site of Commodore John Drake Sloat's landing
in 1846, and where, in fact, Sloat first raised the American flag,
claiming California for the United States. The Custom House
now hosts several local events, including the "Re-enactment of
Sloat's Landing," held in July each year. There is also a small,
worthwhile museum here, which has on display a typical cargo
of a 19th-century merchant ship, comprising pelts, dry goods,
pick-axes and shovels, lanterns, china, cart wheels, and the like.
The museum is open 10-4 daily.

Immediately north of the Custom House, and overlooked by
it, is the colorful old Fisherman's Wharf, with its light-hearted,
haphazard jumble of gift and souvenir shops, kiosks, seafood
restaurants and fish markets. It is an immensely popular tourist
spot, both with adults and children, and a good place to spend
an afternoon. Here you can stroll the piers, with their old
creaking boards, or watch the sea lions that lurk amid the pilings
directly beneath the piers, frequently joined by brown pelicans
— a common sight here — all scavenging for food. From here,
also, you can take sportfishing trips out to sea, or enjoy whale-
watching cruises in season, usually in November. Nearby, at the
Municipal Wharf, it is possible to watch fishing boats as they
unload their catch of the day—salmon, cod, kingfish, herring,
tuna, anchovies. In fact, seven fish processing plants share space
at the end of the wharf, cleaning and packing fish. The wharf
also has good pier fishing, and one or two worthwhile seafood
restaurants.

South of the Custom House, of course, and still on the plaza,
is Pacific House, another old adobe from the Mexican era, with
two stories and a Spanish-style courtyard at the back of it,
featuring a goldfish pool, some ancient shade trees and seasonal
flowers. The adobe dates from the early 1800s, originally built
as a boarding house for seafarers. It now houses a museum, with
several excellent exhibits, representing all four eras of Monterey's history — Indian, Spanish, Mexican and early American
— all arranged by theme and period in a series of rooms.
Museum hours are 10-4, daily.

Nearby, just south of Pacific House, at the edge of the plaza,
is Casa del Oro, yet another delightful Monterey-style adobe,
small, picturesque, dating from 1845 and once used as a gold
depository. Casa del Oro now houses the old Joseph Boston
Store, a gift shop of sorts, featuring Monterey souvenirs and
gifts, cards and books of local historical interest, and fresh herbs
from its small herb garden located adjacent to the store.

Of interest, too, just to the north of the Custom House Plaza

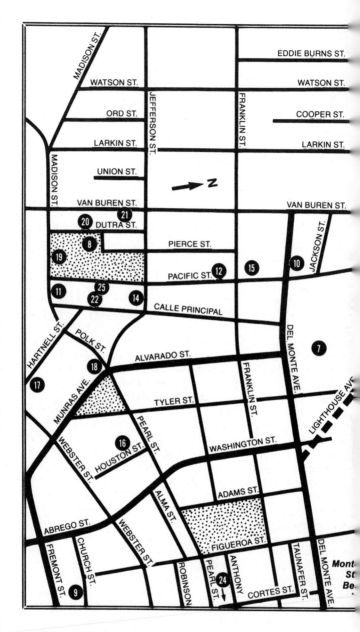

Points of Interest –
1) Monterey Bay Aquarium
2) Custom House
3) Pacific House
4) Fisherman's Wharf
5) Municipal Wharf
6) Coast Guard Wharf
7) Monterey Plaza
   Convention Center
8) Colton Hall
9) Royal Presidio Chapel
10) Casa Soberanes
11) Casa Guiterrez
12) Casa Serrano
13) Casa del Oro
14) Larkin House
15) Merritt House

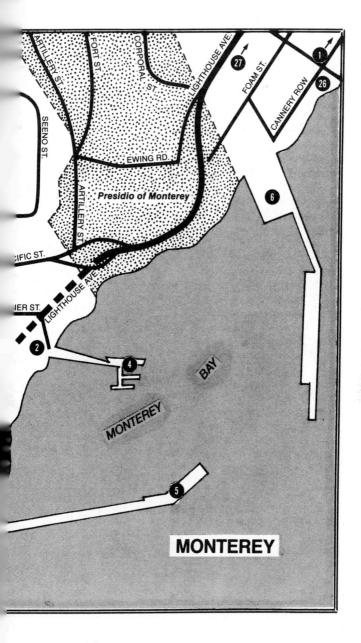

16) Stevenson House
17) Fremont Adobe
18) Cooper-Molera Adobe
19) Underwood-Brown Adobe
20) Vasquez Adobe
21) Alvarado Adobe
22) Maritime Museum

23) First California Theatre
24) Dennis the Menace Playground
25) Monterey Peninsula Museum of Art
26) Historical Wax Museum
27) Pacific Grove

are the First Brick House and the Old Whaling Station, both
dating from 1847, and the latter with a walkway made entirely
from whale vertebrae; and adjoining to the southeast of the
plaza, directly below Pacific House, is the newly-built, yet
delightful, Monterey Convention Center Plaza, not with any
historical merit, but quite in keeping with the Monterey style of
architecture and flavor. The plaza itself is brick-paved, flanked
by the 547-room Doubletree Hotel — one of the largest luxury
hotels in the area — and the 20,000-square-foot convention
center which has in it a ballroom, an exhibition hall, a convention facility with a seating capacity of more than 1500, and
several fine shops and one or two excellent restaurants. The
7-foot bronze statue at the center of the plaza, by the way, is that
of Captain Don Gaspar de Portola, co-founder of Monterey, who
established here in 1770 the first of California's four Spanish
presidios. Interestingly, the statue was a bicentennial gift to the
City of Monterey, in 1970, from King Juan Carlos I of Spain,
sculpted and cast in the Spanish province of Lerida, birthplace
of Portola.

Below the Monterey Convention Center and Custom House
plazas, Calle Principal and Alvarado Street — two of Monterey's oldest streets — dash off southward into the center of the
city. Alvarado Street, in fact, passes through the heart of the
city's business district, and it has on it a handful of beautifully
restored historic buildings, among them the Jacinto Rodriguez
Adobe (1840s) which now houses the Monterey Peninsula
Chamber of Commerce; Casa Sanchez, a single-story Mexican-
era adobe, built partly in the late 1820s; Casa Alvarado, a larger,
two-story adobe, dating from 1834; and the Mission Revival-
style Berquist Building, dating from 1914 and believed to have
been designed by noted California architect William Weeks.

On Calle Principal, of course, at the south end of the street,
you can visit Casa Gutierrez, originally built in 1841 as a private
residence, and now a charming Spanish-style restaurant with a
courtyard for outdoor dining; and the Allen Knight Maritime
Museum, which has on display several superb maritime artifacts
and exhibits, including large scale models of Sebastian
Vizcaino's ship, *San Diego*, and Commodore Sloat's flagship
Savannah, in which he sailed into Monterey Bay in 1846 to
claim California for the United States. Also on display are
thousands of ship pictures, prints and paintings, old steering
wheels, compasses, bells, lanterns, navigation instruments, ship
name-boards, naval history books, age-old shipping records —
including a number of volumes of old Lloyd's Register — and,
most impressive of all, the original Fresnel Light from the Point
Sur Lighthouse, dating from 1880. Worth visiting, too, just off
Calle Principal, on Jefferson Street, is the splendid, Monterey
Colonial-style Larkin House, a large, two-story adobe, dating

from 1835 and now restored to its former elegance, with original furnishings and period decor. The State Parks Department offers guided tours of the Larkin House during scheduled hours.

Among other historic buildings of interest, just to the south of Alvarado Street and Calle Principal, are the Fremont Adobe on Hartnell Street, dating from the early 1840s and where pioneers Jessie and John Charles Fremont once occupied a wing; and the Stevenson House, located on Houston Street and also dating from 1840, and where, in 1879, Scottish-born writer Robert Louis Stevenson lived briefly while courting his future wife, Fanny Osbourne. Another, the Cooper-Molera Adobe, an excellent example of the Monterey-Colonial architectural style and quite possibly one of the largest walled-in complexes in Old Monterey — encompassing roughly 2½ acres — is situated at the corner of Munras and Polk streets. The Cooper-Molera Adobe dates from the late 1820s, and has been largely restored; it now houses an interpretive center, a small bookstore, and a museum. Also try to see the Royal Presidio Chapel, farther to the southeast on Church Street. It dates from 1795 and is claimed to be the oldest existing building in Monterey, still in use.

There remain yet other places of interest in Old Monterey, chiefly historic buildings and old adobes, mostly located along the north-south Pacific Street, which runs more or less parallel to Calle Principal and Alvarado Street, journeying north to Artillery Street — at the corner of which rises the Presidio hill — then on toward Cannery Row. Among the points of interest here is a small, well-preserved section of Old Monterey, wedged between Pacific and Dutra streets, with Jefferson and Madison streets to the north and south of it, respectively. Here you can visit the Alvarado and Vasquez adobes, both dating from the 1830s), the Underwood-Brown Adobe (1834), the Old Monterey Jail (1854), Gordon House (circa 1850), Casa de la Torre (1842), and, best of all, Colton Hall, dating from 1848 and considered to be among America's most distinguished historic buildings. Colton Hall, interestingly, was originally built as a school by Walter Colton, U.S. Navy Chaplain under Commodore Sloat in 1846, and later on Monterey's first mayor and newspaper publisher. In 1849, the building was also the site of California's first Constitutional Convention, where 48 delegates from all parts of the state gathered to draft, debate and ratify a constitution for the proposed State of California. Colton Hall now houses Monterey's city offices on its first floor, with a museum on the second floor, where you can visit the original meeting room in which the delegates gathered in 1849 for the Constitutional Convention, and also view some rare, old documents. The musuem is open 10-4 daily.

North of Colton Hall and the surrounding historic buildings, still on Pacific Street, are the Capitular Hall, dating from 1834;

Casa Serrano, originally built in 1845 and restored, in 1959, to its former glory; the Merritt House, a two-story adobe, dating from the late 1830s and once the residence of Monterey's first judge Josiah Merritt; and Casa Soberanes, one of the loveliest of Monterey's old adobes, dating from the 1840s, and where you can also tour some beautifully-kept 19th-century gardens. Casa Soberanes as well as the other buildings are open to public tours during scheduled hours.

North still, at the corner of Pacific and Scott streets, and well worth visiting, is California's First Theater, originally built in 1846 by a Scottish seafarer, Jack Swan, as a boarding house-cum-tavern and theater, and where the New York Volunteers first began staging plays in 1850. Theater groups still perform here on weekends in summer, offering a variety of 19th-century melodrama and comedy, and Jack Swan's Tavern, too, remains open to the public.

Two other places of interest, a little to the northwest of the theater on Van Buren Street, are the Doud House, a New England- style wooden structure, dating from the 1860s; and the Mayo Hayes O'Donnell Library, originally built in 1876 as the St. James Episcopal Church, Monterey's first Protestant church, and, in 1970, acquired and converted into a library by the Monterey History and Art Association.

A little farther, just to the north of Old Monterey on Pacific Street, lies Monterey's historic Presidio, the oldest of California's four Spanish presidios, which sits hugely on a hilltop overlooking the bay. At the base of the hill, near the corner of Pacific and Artillery streets, is the site of the landing of Captain Don Gaspar de Portola and Father Junipero Serra in 1770. Portola, of course, founded the Monterey Presidio, and Father Serra established here the second of California's 21 Franciscan missions, which, a year later, in 1771, was moved to its present location in Carmel. In any case, within the Presidio are a small military museum, with displays and artifacts depicting the history of Presidio Hill during the Indian, Spanish, Mexican and American eras; the site of Fort Mervine, a harbor fortification built in 1846 by the U.S. Army; the site of El Castillo, a little fortress built by the Spanish government in 1792; and two monuments—one dedicated to Father Serra, and the other, a huge granite memorial, to Commodore John Drake Sloat, commemorating his landing in Monterey and the subsequent American takeover of California in 1846. The Presidio is now home to the Defense Language Institute, one of the largest such language schools in the world, with an average daily enrollment of over 3300. Thirty-five different languages are taught at the Institute by more than 400 instructors, most of whom are natives of the countries whose languages they teach. The Presidio is open to the public.

Also worth visiting, while in the area, are Dennis the Menace Playground at Lake El Estero, just east of Old Monterey, which has several delightful games and mazes for children, designed by Hank Ketchum, local resident and creator of the *Dennis the Menace* comic strip; and the Naval Postgraduate School, a little to the east of Lake El Estero, lying largely between Del Monte Avenue and the highway (1), and where you can view the old, 19th-century adobe buildings which once housed the Hotel Del Monte, claimed during the late 1800s and early 1900s to be one of the most luxurious hotel resorts on the West Coast, visited by such personalities of the day as Andrew Carnegie, William Vanderbilt, Chauncey Depew, Joseph Pulitzer, Mary Pickford and Will Rogers, among others. The old Del Monte buildings now house the living quarters, classrooms and administrative offices of the Naval Postgraduate School.

Cannery Row

Adjoining to the northwest of Old Monterey and Fisherman's Wharf is Cannery Row, the great glory of Monterey, stretching a mile or so from the Coast Guard Station in the east to more or less the outskirts of neighboring Pacific Grove. This, in fact, is the Cannery Row of John Steinbeck fame, romanticized in his classic of the same name — *Cannery Row*—as "a poem, a stink, a grating noise." Starting at the turn of the century, several sardine canning factories located along this row, peaking to over sixteen in the 1930s; and scores of bawdy, raucous fishermen, eccentrics, and other interesting characters were attracted here as well, many of whom Steinbeck encountered during his visit to the row, and who later became the inspiration for his novels *Tortilla Flats* (1935), *Cannery Row* (1945) and *Sweet Thursday* (1945). Most of the canneries, of course, closed in the late 1940s, and many of them, in the following years, fell into disrepair or disappeared from the scene altogether, gutted by fire.

In recent years, however, Cannery Row has witnessed a resurgence of sorts with renewed interest and new investment, restoring or remodelling and converting many of the old, surviving canneries and other buildings into colorful little malls, with fine shops, galleries, restaurants and games arcades. The Cannery Row Trading Company building, for instance, now houses shops and restaurants and a gallery; the Enterprise Cannery houses a gallery, a furniture showroom and offices; the Aenas Sardine Products Building, dating from 1944 and featuring an overpass, has in it an antique store; the Bear Flag Building, dating from 1929 and once used as a brothel, now houses a series of shops, offices and eating establishments, and a gallery; the Del Mar Canning Company is now home to a restaurant, the

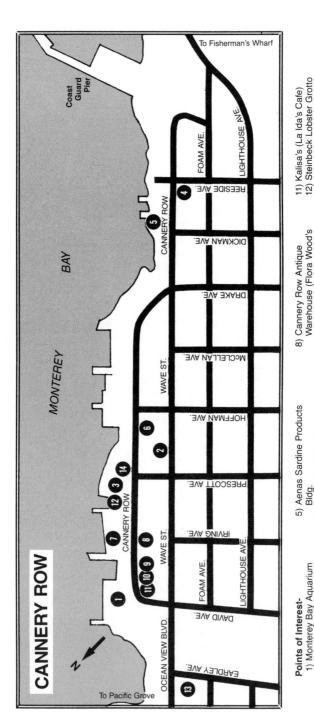

CANNERY ROW

To Fisherman's Wharf

Coast Guard Pier

MONTEREY BAY

MONTEREY

To Pacific Grove

Points of Interest-
1) Monterey Bay Aquarium
2) Edgewater Packing Co.
3) Monterey Canning Co.
4) Enterprise Cannery
5) Aenas Sardine Products Bldg.
6) Bear Flag Bldg. & Captain's Cove
7) 800 Cannery Row
8) Cannery Row Antique Warehouse (Flora Wood's Lone Star Cafe)
9) Cannery Row Trading Co.
10) Wing Chong Building
11) Kalisa's (La Ida's Cafe)
12) Steinbeck Lobster Grotto (Del Mar Canning Co.)
13) American Tin Cannery
14) John Steinbeck's Bust

Steinbeck Lobster Grotto; and the Edgewater Packing Company building has in it some shops, a restaurant, and an arcade with a 1905 carousel with hand-carved horses, and other carnival games and food concessions. Another, the Monterey Canning Company building, one of the only cannery buildings with its original overpass, houses an assortment of shops, galleries and restaurants, and also wine tasting rooms for the Bargetto and Paul Masson wineries, the latter with a wine museum and an antique corkscrew collection on display. In the Monterey Canning Company building, too, is the Spirit of Monterey Wax Museum, especially interesting to first-time visitors to the row, featuring more than 100 lifesize figures, many of them models of Steinbeck's characters, including the marine biologist "Doc" Ricketts, the most famous of all, and Lee Chong, Sam Mally and Dora Flood. A few of Steinbeck's locales, described in his novels, can also be visited on Cannery Row, among them the Pacific Biological Laboratories at 800 Cannery Row, originally Doc Ricketts' marine laboratory; the Cannery Row Antique Warehouse at 700 Cannery Row, which, in *Cannery Row*, was Dora Flood's bordello; Lee Chong's Heavenly Flower Grocery at 835 Cannery Row, owned by Lee Chong in Steinbeck's novel; and Kalisa's at 851 Cannery Row, which, in *Sweet Thursday*, was "La Ida's Cafe."

Also to be recommended to visitors to the area is the Monterey Bay Aquarium — quite possibly Monterey's greatest tourist attraction — located at the west end of Cannery Row, at the site of the old Hovden Cannery. The aquarium was originally built in 1981, at a cost of around $40 million, and is one of the largest of its kind in the nation — comprising more than 220,000 square feet. It has in it over 6500 sea creatures, representing some 525 species of fish, mammals, invertebrates, birds and plants, all native to Monterey Bay. The aquarium's chief attraction, of course, is its 335,000-gallon living kelp forest exhibit, which rises three stories — 28 feet — believed to be the tallest aquarium exhibit in the world. Another, a 90-foot-long, 335,000-gallon exhibit recreates the deep reefs and sandy sea floors of the bay, and contains in it sharks of all sizes, bat rays and several other open-ocean fish. There is, besides, a sea otter exhibit here, quite popular with both adults and children, and several petting pools, an aquaculture laboratory, and countless marine exhibits, highlighting native sea life. A walk-through aviary, another well-liked aquarium exhibit, features a variety of birds inhabiting the Monterey Bay shore and marshlands; from here, too, you can view Stanford University's Hopkins Marine Station, an educational and research facility established in 1891 for the study of intertidal life, situated just to the west of the aquarium. There is also a gift-cum-book shop on the premises, as well as a cafeteria. The Monterey Bay Aquarium is open to the public daily, and there is an admission fee.

Close at hand, too, just to the southwest of the aquarium, and also well worth visiting, is the American Tin Cannery, formerly the American Can Company — a manufacturing facility for sardine cans during the 1930s and 1940s — and now a superb shopping mall, housing an assortment of fine shops and restaurants. The American Tin Cannery, however, is located just outside the Monterey city limits, in neighboring Pacific Grove.

Seaside, Del Rey Oaks, Sand City, Ford Ord and Marina

Immediately northeast of Monterey lies Seaside, founded in 1890 by Dr. John Roberts, a memorable Monterey Peninsula pioneer, who made house calls on horseback along the rugged Big Sur coast during the early 1900s, and who, some years later, also mapped the wild, untamed country between Monterey and San Luis Obispo — on foot! Roberts Lake, situated along the southwestern edge of Seaside, between Del Monte Avenue and Highway 1, is named for Dr. Roberts.

Of interest, too, at Seaside, are the City Hall on Harcourt Avenue, believed to have been designed by noted architect Edward Durrell Stone, and which has changing art exhibits on display; and the Monterey Peninsula Buddhist Temple on Noche Buena, where a "Bonsai Show" is held in May each year. Also try to see the St. Seraphim's Russian Orthodox Church at Francis Avenue and Canyon Del Rey, just to the south of the Seaside City Hall, originally built in the early 1950s at the site of the city's first post office, and characteristic in its Slavic architecture.

Just east of Seaside, nestled along Monterey Bay, is tiny Sand City, a mile wide and one and one-half miles long, notable as the second smallest incorporated city in California; and south of Seaside, directly above the Monterey Peninsula Airport, sits Del Rey Oaks, comprising all of 286 acres. At Del Rey Oaks there is a small, 34-acre park, located more or less in the center of the city, which has a golf driving range, tennis courts, a ball field, and a recreation building.

Adjoining to the east of Seaside, of course, is Fort Ord, encompassing some 28,500 acres, and home to nearly 25,000 military personnel. Fort Ord was originally founded as an Army base in 1917, and named for the illustrious Major General Edward Otho Cresap Ord, a decorated Civil War hero, and who once also served under John Charles Fremont as a lieutenant. Fort Ord, over the years, has served as a training area for troops deployed during World War II, as well as a basic training camp for recruits for the Vietnam and Korean wars. The military installation now has theaters, libraries, service clubs, a hospital, and a wide range of facilities for both indoor and outdoor sports.

Finally, directly north of Seaside, Sand City and Fort Ord lies Marina, the third largest city in the area, and in many ways the "Gateway to the Monterey Peninsula." Marina is notable mainly for its abundant, fine sand dunes, which offer some excellent hang- gliding possibilities. There is also an undeveloped beach area here, the Salinas River State Beach, lying a little way to the north of Marina, and which, again, has sand dunes and a beach that extends almost to the outskirts of Moss Landing, farther north. The Salinas River State Beach is located just off Potrero Road, which goes off Highway 1.

PACIFIC GROVE

Pacific Grove, adjoining to the west of Monterey, is a pictur-esque little coastal town, originally founded in 1875 as a Meth-odist seaside resort. The town is abundant in brightly colored Victorian homes — quite in contrast to Monterey's Spanish-style adobes — and notable, too, as "Butterfly Town, USA," where millions on Monarch butterflies migrate for the winter, usually arriving in October. The orange-black butterflies can be seen — in season — in the Butterfly Trees Park just to the northwest of town, near the corner of Lighthouse Avenue and Alder Street, hanging like dried leaves from the "butterfly trees." The town also hosts a Butterfly Parade in October each year, to celebrate the Monarch migration.

Pacific Grove's Victorians, of course, can be seen throughout town, especially concentrated on Lighthouse and Central ave-nues and along the waterfront. Of particular interest are the beautifully restored Queen Anne Victorians, Gosby House Inn and Maison Bergerac, both located on Lighthouse Avenue, ad-jacent to one another, dating from 1887 and 1892, respectively. Among other buildings of note are the Pryor House on Ocean View Boulevard, dating from 1908 and once the home of Pacific Grove mayor John Pryor; the Green Gables, a Swiss Gothic, built in 1888 and now a bed and breakfast inn, located at the corner of Ocean View Boulevard and Fifth Street; and The Centrella, situated on Central Avenue. This last, the Centrella, is perhaps the finest of them all, a thoroughly enchanting bed and breakfast establishment, dating from 1889, and recently, in 1981, restored to its former splendor, at a cost of around $1 million. Many of the town's other Victorians are also quite lovely, with their multi-colored shutters and doors, and some actually date from over a century, to when the town was first founded, in 1875. There are, in fact, over 180 homes in Pacific Grove built prior to 1890, and on the two-day "Victorian House Tours," held in March each year, visitors can view most of these

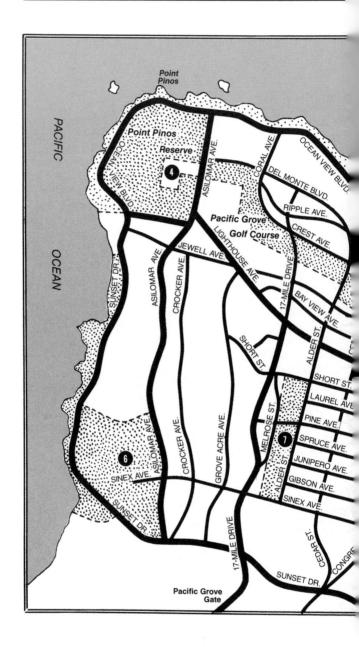

Points of Interest-
1) Lover's Point Park
2) Pacific Grove Art Center
3) Museum of Natural History
4) Point Pinos Lighthouse
5) The Centrella Hotel
6) Asilomar State Beach & Convention Center
7) Butterfly Trees Park

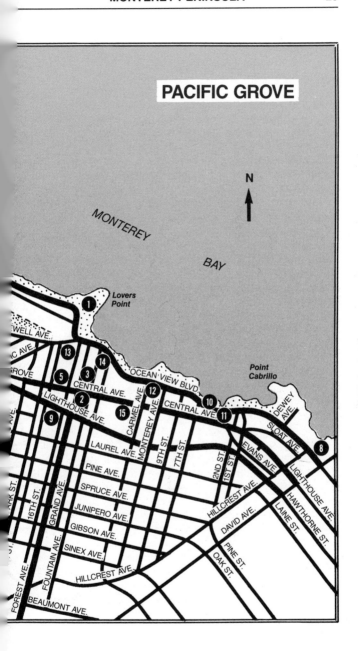

PACIFIC GROVE

8) American Tin Cannery
9) Gosby House Inn
10) Green Gables Inn
11) Martine Inn

12) Pryor House
13) McCoy House
14) House of Seven Gables
15) St. Mary's Church

turn-of-the-century homes, a fair number of them restored to their former elegance.

Pacific Grove also enjoys a beautiful coastline, with many miles of oceanside walks. Lover's Point Park, by the ocean by Pacific Avenue and Ocean View Boulevard, is especially popular with walkers and joggers, and a good place for ocean-gazing. The park also has picnicking, swimming and bird-watching possibilities, and is a departure point for scuba divers. Besides which, in July each year, Lover's Point is the site of a grand fireworks display, part of the "Feast of Lanterns" — a local festival that recounts a Chinese legend about a Mandarin's daughter who runs away with her peasant lover to drown herself, and the ensuing search for her by the villagers, in lighted boats with lanterns. The week-long festival features a lighted-boats parade, a lantern procession, the crowning of Queen Topaz, and, finally, a fireworks display.

On the coast too, is the Point Pinos Reserve, with an ancient lighthouse, built in 1855 and believed to be the oldest continuously operating lighthouse on the West Coast, with its original fresnel lenses and prisms still in use. There is a small museum here, open to the public, devoted entirely to Coast Guard history.

Another place of interest, much to be recommended to first-time visitors, is Pacific Grove's Natural History Museum on Central Avenue, which has displays of more than 400 species of birds from Monterey County, as well as exhibits depicting the animal, vegetable and mineral life of the Monterey Peninsula area. The museum also has an excellent relief map of Monterey Bay, in which you can see the great chasm in the bay, plunging, in just a few miles, from some 300 feet to over 8,400 feet!

Try to also visit the Pacific Grove Art Center on Lighthouse Avenue, where, in a Victorian setting, paintings, sculpture, graphics and historical photographs are displayed in galleries and studios. The art center is open to public viewing during weekdays.

Of interest, too, at the west end of Pacific Grove on Asilomar Boulevard is the Asilomar Conference Center — a 105-acre beachfront conference center, backed by forest land, and designated a National Historic Landmark. The center has 48 meeting rooms, 313 overnight guest rooms, a heated swimming pool, and volleyball, golf and tennis facilities close at hand. The Asilomar Beach, of course, has some tidepools, and picnicking and surfing possibilities.

PEBBLE BEACH

Pebble Beach, famous the world over as the home of golf, lies directly to the south of Pacific Grove. It is, of course, itself

ontained in the fabulous, 8,400-acre Del Monte Forest, and
djoined to its west by the Pacific Ocean and to the southeast by
Carmel and the largely pastoral Carmel Valley. There are in
Pebble Beach no fewer than seven superb, world-class golf
ourses, many in spectacular, oceanfront settings; besides which
Pebble Beach also has in it the fabled 17-Mile Drive, an
stonishingly scenic drive, billed as "the slowest way between
Monterey and Carmel," which passes by some of the most
photographed coastal scenery in the world—featuring sandy,
white-foam beaches and small, sheltered coves, cliff-top fairways and picturesque groves of gnarled Monterey Cypress, sea
ion colonies and wild, shore bird habitats — as well as some of
he most magnificent palatial estates on the West Coast.

There are four gates by which to enter Pebble Beach on the
17-Mile Drive; two at Pacific Grove, another on Highway 1, and
he fourth at the south end, at Carmel. There is an admission fee
charged at the point of entry, of around $6.00 per car, and a map
pinpointing all the places of interest enroute is also available at
he gate.

Although it is possible to select any one of the four points of
entry to Pebble Beach, let us, for the purposes of our tour, begin
at the Pacific Grove gate, and journey south. Just a half-mile
from Pacific Grove, northernmost on the 17-Mile Drive, is the
lovely Spanish Bay, with a resort of the same name — one of
the newest developments in the area — comprising a 270-room
luxury hotel, and an 18-hole, championship golf course with a
clubhouse and several fine shops and a restaurant or two. Spanish Bay, interestingly, is also the site of Monterey's co-founder,
Gaspar de Portola's landing in 1769, and where, in fact, Portola
camped during his first, unsuccessful attempt to locate Monterey
Bay. Portola, of course, returned the following year, on his
second expedition, and found Monterey Bay farther to the north.

Just to the south of Spanish Bay, another half-mile or so is
Point Joe, which, in the early days, sailors mistakenly thought
to be the entrance to Monterey Bay, resulting in several shipwrecks on the rocks just offshore. Nearby, too, just off Point Joe,
you can see the "Restless Sea," one of the few places in the world
where ocean currents meet, creating turbulence even on calm
days.

South still, below Point Joe, is the Monterey Peninsula Coun-
try Club, formerly the site of the Bing Crosby National Pro-Am
Tournament. The club has two excellent 18-hole courses: The
Dunes Course, which first opened for play in 1925, and the
Shore Course, completed in 1963. The courses, however, are
private, not open to the public.

Continuing on the 17-Mile Drive, near the southern end of
the Monterey Peninsula Country Club's Shore Course, just offshore, are the Bird Rock and Seal Rock, where you can view

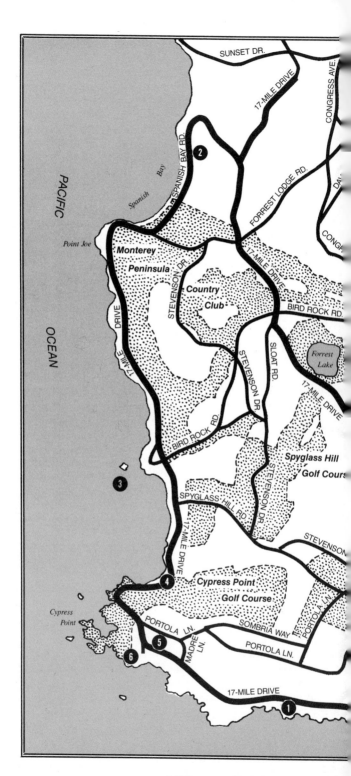

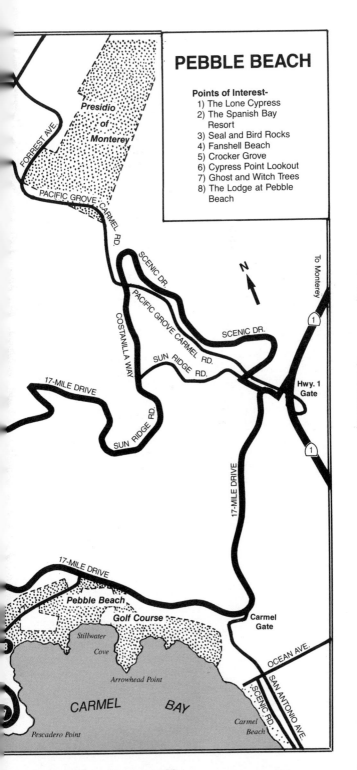

PEBBLE BEACH

Points of Interest-
1) The Lone Cypress
2) The Spanish Bay Resort
3) Seal and Bird Rocks
4) Fanshell Beach
5) Crocker Grove
6) Cypress Point Lookout
7) Ghost and Witch Trees
8) The Lodge at Pebble Beach

countless seagulls, black cormorants and other shoreline birds in their natural habitat, as well as herds of sealions, sea otters and the smaller leopard and harbor seals, lurking in the waters below. There is a popular little picnic area here, with tables and benches, and good views of the wildlife.

A little way from the picnic area at the Bird and Seal rocks just to the south, Spyglass Hill Road peels from the 17-Mile Drive and dashes off southeastward to the Spyglass Hill Golf Course, site of the annual AT&T Pebble Beach National Pro-Am Tournament, and ranked among the top 40 courses in the country. The Spyglass Hill course was built in 1966, and is open to the public. There is a small snack bar here as well, serving sandwiches and soft drinks, overlooking the 9th hole. Spyglass Hill, besides, also has its associations with Robert Louis Stevenson, who used the area as a model for the descriptions in his classic, *Treasure Island*. Interestingly, each of the holes at the Spyglass Hill Golf Course is named after a character from Stevenson's book, such as "Long John Silver," "Jim Hawkins," and the like.

Returning to our main route of travel, however, a half-mile south of the Spyglass Hill Road intersection is the lovely crescent-shaped, white-sand Fanshell Beach, and just to the southwest of there, jutting out into the ocean, is Cypress Point, with a lookout that offers some of the finest, unobstructed views of both the Pebble Beach coastline to the north and Carmel Bay and the northern portion of the Big Sur coastline to the south. On clear days, you can even see the Point Sur Lighthouse, some 20 miles to the south. Here, too, quite close to Cypress Point is the Cypress Point Golf Course, a private course, built in 1928 and ranked among the top 20 courses in the United States, especially notable for its 16th green, which can only be reached by driving over some 200 yards of open ocean! Also of interest here, directly below the golf course, is the Crocker Grove, a 13-acre reserve containing native Monterey Cypress, believed to be among the largest and oldest on the peninsula.

Farther still, another half-mile or so southeastward along the coast is the Lone Cypress, one of the Monterey Peninsula's most famous landmarks, clinging to virtually bare rock, overlooking the ocean. Not far from there, about a mile down the coast at Pescadero Point are the Ghost and Witch trees, two dramatic Monterey Cypress, with trunks bleached white by the wind and sea spray, described by Robert Louis Stevenson as "ghosts fleeing before the wind." At Pescadero Point, too, on foggy nights, we are told, you can see the ghost of Maria del Carmel Garcia Barreto Madariaga — who once owned (and twice sold) the Rancho El Pescadero which was situated along the coast here — wandering near the Ghost and Witch trees.

In any event, north from Pescadero Point, a little way, is the

ebble Beach resort, the oldest and best-known resort in the
rea, with a notable lodge with luxury guest accommodations,
restaurants, several fine shops, tennis courts, and even an eques-
ian center with more than 34 miles of bridle trails. There is also
 superb, 18-hole golf course here, built in 1919, and which was
e site of the 1972 and 1982 U.S. Open Golf Tournments, as
ell as the 1977 PGA Championship. In 1992, Pebble Beach
ill once again host the U.S. Open. The golf course, by the way,
 open to the public.

From the Pebble Beach Lodge you have a choice of routes.
ou can either proceed directly east, then south, briefly, to leave
e 17-Mile Drive by way of the Carmel gate, or continue on the
op northward past the Highway 1 gate and the Shepherd's
noll Vista Point which has excellent, all-round views of Mon-
erey Bay and the San Gabilan Mountains beyond; then south
nd northwestward again toward Spanish Bay, passing by Huck-
eberry Hill — one of the highest points in the Del Monte Forest
— and the Poppy Hills Golf Course, home to the Northern
California Golf Association. From Spanish Bay, of course, you
an exit via the Pacific Grove gate at the north end of Pebble
Beach.

CARMEL-BY-THE-SEA

Carmel — pronounced, by the way, Car-*mel*, and meaning "at
rest" — has the charm and gentility of an English village. It is
small, rural, dignified, and yet a stunningly beautiful town, less
than one mile square and situated on a splendid, forested coastal
slope at the southern tip of the Monterey Peninsula — at the
head of Carmel Bay. Its fame, of course, lies in its superb
shopping district, where people from all over the country go —
just to shop! But to simply say that Carmel is a fine place for
shopping is to greatly understate the case. For here, within some
four square blocks are clustered an astonishing 150 shops and
more than 90 art galleries (not to mention at least 60 restaurants
featuring almost every type of known cuisine)! The variety in
the shopping is just as amazing: here you can buy everything
from Gucci fashionwear to African tribal masks, from Charles
Wysocki oils to Ansel Adams composites, from safari clothing
to fine furs, from imported china and Wedgewood crystal to
vegetable-dye Tibetan rugs and handcrafted, south-of-the-bor-
der pottery. Indeed, the shops here offer a startling variety, from
locally-made gifts to handicrafts from far away lands, and art
galleries display an equally wide spectrum of works, from those
of resident artists to those of the internationally acclaimed, with
prices ranging from modest to mind-boggling. But even more

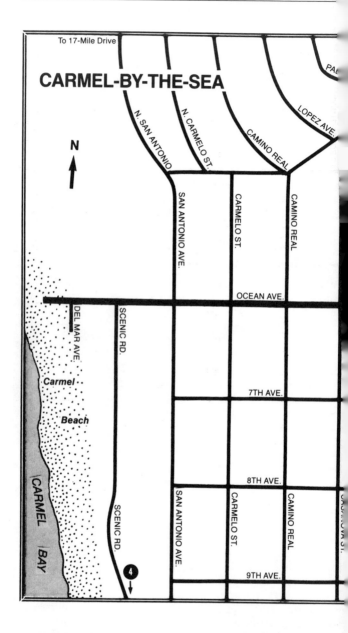

Points of Interest -
1) Carmel Mission
2) Carmel Plaza
3) Sunset Center
4) Tor House
5) Hog's Breath Inn
6) Tuck Box English Tea House

7) Carmel Art Association Galleries
8) The Weston Gallery
9) Photography West
10) GWS Gallery
11) Bleich of Carmel
12) Bill W. Dodge Gallery
13) Hanson Gallery

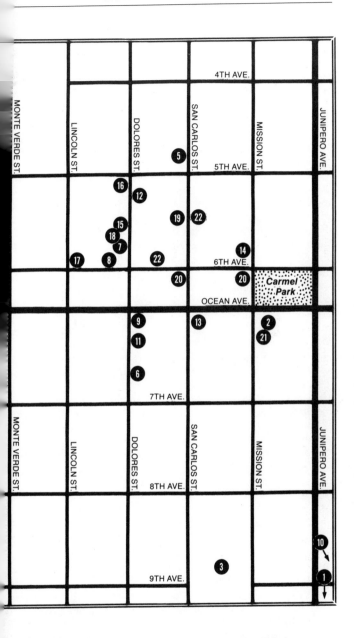

14) Cottage Gallery
15) Highlands Gallery
16) Lindsey Gallery
17) Gallery Americana
18) First Impressions

19) Walter White Galleries
20) Zantman Galleries
21) Casa Dolores
22) Simic Galleries

than the shopping possibilities, it is the shopping district itself that is most remarkable — rural, wooded and utterly charming with shops tucked away among age-old shade trees which, on larger perspective, are part of an unrestrained urban forest that requires four full-time city employees to maintain — a situation that owes something to a 1916 ordinance, banning the cutting of trees.

In any case, Ocean Avenue, quite lovely with its multifarious shade trees, shrubs and flower beds, is probably the town's most important street, with the majority of the chain and department stores situated along it, as well as the beautiful Carmel Plaza which has some thirty or so fine shops and restaurants — including such well-known names as Saks Fifth Avenue, I Magnin and Banana Republic. Other streets in the shopping district include Dolores, San Carlos, Mission and Lincoln, and Fifth, Sixth and Seventh avenues. On Dolores, between Fifth and Sixth, lies Carmel's self-styled "Gallery Row," with more than a dozen art galleries to be found there, among them the Carmel Art Association Galleries, the most prestigious of all, where you can view the works of professional, local artists, displayed in eight different rooms, with exhibits changing every month. Also try to visit the Weston Gallery on Sixth, between Dolores and Lincoln streets, which has some original works of Ansel Adams and other noted 20th-century photographers; and south of Ocean Avenue on Dolores you can search out the Tuckbox English Tea House, housed in an enchanting little Doll House-style cottage, with a thatched roof and Tudor exterior.

On San Carlos Street, between Fifth and Sixth, is the Hog's Breath Inn, an essentially American-style restaurant, owned in part by actor Clint Eastwood, and now a favorite tourist haunt. Open for lunch and dinner, it has both courtyard and indoor dining, with fireplaces and a rustic, casual atmosphere. On the menu are such entrees as the Dirty Harry Burger, Enforcer Burger, Mysterious Misty and the Eiger Sandwich, reminiscent of Eastwood's most memorable films.

If you are in the area during the summer months (usually around July-August), try to attend Carmel's annual Bach Festival at the Sunset Center on San Carlos Street. It is one of the most notable classical music events on the Monterey Peninsula. Another, the small, open-air Forest Theater at the south-eastern edge of town, also schedules some theater performances in season; for a schedule, call the theater at (408) 649-5561.

West of town, at the bottom end of Ocean Avenue lies the spectacular Carmel Beach, with white sand and foaming surf, and framed by dark, twisty Monterey cypress. It is a popular place for strolling, picnicking and ocean viewing, although swimming is not particularly encouraged due to the shifting currents and the cold water. Just to the south of the beach a

ile-long scenic drive journeys along the head of Carmel Bay
lead to the Carmel Point State Beach, passing by, along the
ay, the picturesque, native-stone Tor House, formerly the home
f California poet Robinson Jeffers, who built it with his own
ands., between 1918- 1930, from stones taken largely from the
Carmel Beach, as well as from the Great Wall of China, the
Pyramid of Cheops and Hadrian's Villa. The Tor House also has
a secret staircase in its 40-foot Hawk Tower, and an ancient
porthole between the second and third floors, reported to have
come from the ship on which Napoleon escaped from Elba in
1815. Tours of the house are available by appointment, in small
groups.

South of Carmel also, on a small rise, overlooking the Carmel
River, is the Basilica San Carlos Borromeo del Rio Carmelo —
or the Carmel Mission — originally built in 1770 in Monterey,
and moved to its present site the following year, in 1771. The
mission has a delightful courtyard, filled with California pop-
pies and other flowers, as in season, and a museum with displays
of mission relics which include the original silver altar brought
across by Father Junipero Serra, founder of the mission, from
Baja California. Fathers Serra and Lasuen — each of whom
founded nine California missions — and Father Crespi, are
buried in the mission.

CARMEL VALLEY

Carmel Valley, once described by Robert Louis Stevenson as
"a true California valley," lies largely to the southeast of the
Carmel Village and Highway 1, extending some 14 miles or so
inland, along the Carmel River, encompassing roughly 65,000
acres of pastureland, ranches and orchards, overlooked by gentle, oak-studded hills. The valley is, of course, primarily rural,
but still with something in it of visitor interest. Near the mouth
of the valley, for instance, just off Carmel Valley Road — which
goes off Highway 1 eastward, passing through the heart of the
valley — are a handful of interesting little shopping centers,
among them the celebrated "Barnyard," a unique shopping complex with some 55 shops, boutiques, galleries and restaurants —
including the popular Thunderbird Bookshop and Cafe —
housed in nine picturesque old barns, and surrounded by lavish
flower gardens, overflowing with seasonal color. Other shopping centers of interest here include the Crossroads Shopping
Center, the Carmel Rancho Center and the Carmel Center, all
situated within easy distance of each other.

Inland a little way from The Barnyard and the other shopping
centers are the Rancho Canada Golf Club and the Carmel Valley

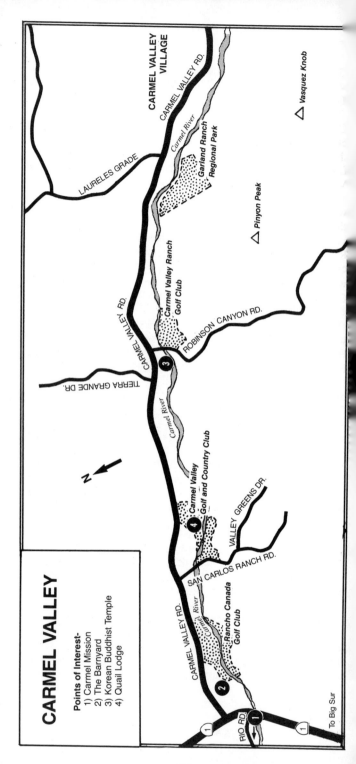

CARMEL VALLEY

Points of Interest-

1) Carmel Mission
2) The Barnyard
3) Korean Buddhist Temple
4) Quail Lodge

CARMEL VALLEY VILLAGE

CARMEL VALLEY RD.

LAURELES GRADE

Carmel River

Garland Ranch Regional Park

△ Vasquez Knob

△ Pinyon Peak

Carmel Valley Ranch Golf Club

CARMEL VALLEY RD.

ROBINSON CANYON RD.

TIERRA GRANDE DR.

Carmel River

Carmel Valley Golf and Country Club

VALLEY GREENS DR.

SAN CARLOS RANCH RD.

CARMEL VALLEY RD.

Carmel River

Rancho Canada Golf Club

RIO RD.

To Big Sur

N

Golf and Country Club, located just to the south of Carmel Valley Road, and sprawled on both sides of the Carmel River. The Rancho Canada club has two 18-hole courses, the West Course and the East Course, both open to the public; and at the Carmel Valley Golf Club, too, there is an excellent, 18-hole championship course, besides which the club has, adjacent to it, the well-known — and architecturally interesting — Quail Lodge, with its five-star, luxury accommodations. The Carmel Valley Golf Club, however, is not open to the public.

Another golf club, the Carmel Valley Ranch Golf Club, also with an 18-hole course, is located a few miles farther on, near the intersection of Carmel Valley Road and the Robinson Canyon Road which dashes off southward, crossing over the Carmel River. On Robinson Canyon Road, also, southward from the golf course, is the Korean Buddhist Temple, a lovely, Oriental wooden structure, situated on a 7½-acre site, overlooking the Carmel River. The temple is open to the public during Sunday services.

Nearby, too, and well worth visiting, is the Chateau Julien winery, located on Carmel Valley Road, some 5 miles from the Highway 1 intersection. The winery is housed in a charming, French chateau-style building, and is open to the public for wine tasting and retail sales. Another valley winery, the Robert Talbott Winery, lies farther inland, several miles southeastward on Carmel Valley Road; it, too, can be visited by appointment.

Eastward still, some 8 miles from Highway 1, near the intersection of Carmel Valley Road and the mountainous Los Laureles Grade which journeys northward to merge with the Monterey-Salinas Highway, is the 540-acre Garland Ranch Regional Park, with picnicking, fishing, horseback riding and bird-watching possibilities, and more than 7 miles of nature walks, some of them indeed quite scenic, meandering through meadows awash with wildflowers, or climbing to mountain peaks, with superb, all-round views. Trail maps are available at the visitor center, located just inside the park.

Some 4 miles or so farther inland on Carmel Valley Road lies the Carmel Valley Village, a small, rural community, with very little to interest the visitor, except its Hidden Valley Opera Theater, located just to the west of the village on Ford Road, and where music seminars are held during the summer months.

Beyond the Carmel Village, of course, the Carmel Valley Road continues southeastward several miles, journeying through wild, wooded country, to finally emerge on Highway 101, some 12 miles south of Soledad.

POINT LOBOS STATE RESERVE

Point Lobos State Reserve — which derives its name from *Punta de los Lobos Marinos*, Spanish for "Point of the Sea-wolves" — lies at the southern tip of Carmel Bay, some 2 or 3 miles south of Carmel, comprising the land mass jutting out northwestward into the ocean. It is of course one of the most beautiful nature reserves on the California coast, and a superb outdoor museum, where you can visit sea lion and sea otter colonies and brown pelican breeding grounds, as well as a half-mile stretch of some of the oldest and loveliest Monterey Cypress on the peninsula. The reserve itself encompasses approximately 1,250 acres, 750 acres of which lie submerged, forming what is considered to be the first undersea Ecological Reserve in the country. There are also a handful of small beaches here, and several miles of nature trails, meandering quite enchantingly through the reserve. At Whalers Cove, which is located along the northeastern end of the reserve, and which is also the site of an 1860s Portugese whaling station, you can even launch boats; and at China Cove, at the southern end of the park, swimming is permitted. Point Lobos, besides, has some picnicking and scuba diving possibilities as well, and is a good place for whale watching during the annual, 12,000-mile whale migration, usually around November. The park is open 9 a.m.-7 p.m. daily, and there is an admission fee charged at the gate.

BIG SUR

South from the Point Lobos State Reserve lies Big Sur, a spectacular, 90-mile stretch of coastline, extending from just below Point Lobos to the tiny coastal settlements of Big Sur, Lucia, Gorda, and on to San Simeon. Indeed, Big Sur — which derives its name from "El Grande Sur," Spanish for "Big South" — offers in it one of the world's most scenic coastal drives, with dramatic cliffs overhanging sandy beaches and small, rocky coves, and the rugged Santa Lucia Mountains plunging directly into the sea. The highway here — Highway 1, built in 1937 and designated California's first scenic route — clings precariously to the coastline much of the way, dipping and climbing and weaving madly around the coastal hills, treating the motorist-sightseer to endless sweeping views of the ocean.

The Big Sur drive is in fact quite splendid from the moment it sets out, passing by wilderness reserves and state parks, secluded beaches and coves, small, wooded canyons and valleys, and numerous vista-point turnouts all along the highway,

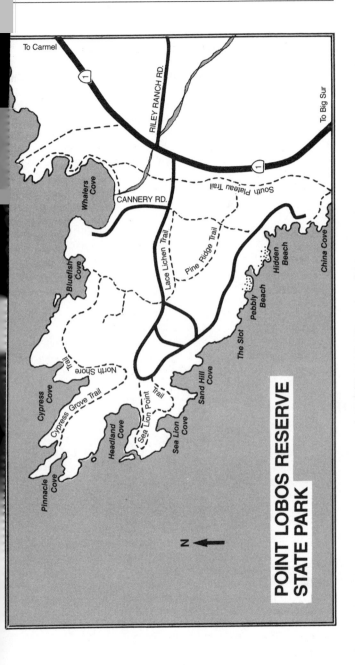

POINT LOBOS RESERVE
STATE PARK

most with superb, breathtaking views. Northernmost, of course
a little way to the south of Point Lobos are Yankee Point, which
has excellent views of the coastline, and is also a good place for
whale-watching (in season); and Soberanes Point, farther to the
south, named for some of the early settlers in the area. South of
there, another 2 miles or so, is the Garrapata Beach — pronounced *Gehr-rah-pat-tah*, and meaning "wood tick" — named
for the abundant ticks found in the area by early settlers. Garrapata is a lovely, curved beach, with a path leading down to it
from the highway, and just to the south of it you can see the
Garrapata Creek meandering down to the ocean, crossed over
by a bridge, some 95 feet high, and with a span of 150 feet.

A mile or more from the Garrapata Beach, southward, is
Rocky Point, with a restaurant of the same name, quite popular
with seafood lovers, overlooking the ocean; and just to the south
of there, the narrow, twisty Palo Colorado Road dashes off
inland, down the Palo Colorado Canyon, some 8 miles, to
Bottcher's Gap, a Forest Service area with campsites and a
trailhead for several hiking trails leading into the 159,000-acre
Ventana Wilderness, part of the Los Padres National Forest.
Nearby, also, directly below the intersection of Palo Colorado
Road and Highway 1, is the site of the old Notley's Landing,
from where, during the late 1800s and early 1900s, tanbark and
timber, harvested from the Big Sur hills and canyons, were
shipped. Notley's Landing, more recently, was also the prototype for the setting for the movie, *Sandy's Bride*, starring Liv
Ullman and Gene Hackman. The movie, interestingly, was based
on a novel by Big Sur resident, the late Lillian Bos Ross, entitled
The Stranger.

Not far from the Palo Colorado Canyon, another one and
one-half miles on Highway 1 is the Rocky Creek Bridge which
spans some 240 feet across the mouth of Rocky Creek, and
immediately south of there are Bixby Point and Bixby Bridge,
the latter quite possibly one of the most photographed sights on
the Big Sur coast. Indeed, the Bixby Bridge, built in 1932, was
quite a marvel in its day, claimed, at the time of its construction,
to be the longest concrete arch span bridge in the world, with a
central span of 320 feet, and towering nearly 260 feet above the
Bixby Creek. It is also interesting to note that the main concrete
pillars of the bridge are hollow, with doors located on the
outsides of these, enabling building inspectors to enter the
pillars, directly beneath the bridge, to make safety checks. There
are also observation alcoves located along the bridge at intervals, offering visitors unparalleled views of the Bixby Creek
Canyon and the ocean.

Below Bixby Point, of course, is Hurricane Point, one of the
windiest spots on the coast, a little over a mile distant. It has
excellent views, to the south, of the Little Sur River as it fans

out into the ocean, with a sandy beach and a lagoon located at the mouth of the river; and of Point Sur, farther to the south, where there is an historic lighthouse, perched on a 350-foot-high volcanic rock. The lighthouse dates from 1889, and is still in operation, with its powerful beam visible nearly 25 miles out at sea. There is also a small naval station at the foot of the lighthouse, engaged in oceanographic research. The lighthouse, however, is not open to the public. The Point Sur Lighthouse is more than 3 miles to the south of Hurricane Point, and the mouth of the Little Sur River, roughly one and one-half miles.

From Point Sur, it is another 2 miles, approximately, to the Andrew Molera State Park, a 2,154-acre scenic nature reserve, formerly the Molera Rancheria, lying largely between Highway 1 and the ocean, extending some 2 miles inland along the Big Sur River. The park has several hiking trails meandering through it, both along the river and down toward the sea, besides which, it also has good picnicking, fishing and horseback riding possibilities. Also of interest here is the Old Coast Road which dashes off northward from the top end of the Andrew Molera park, journeying through scenic wooded country and over mountain ridges, to emerge near the Bixby Bridge on Highway 1.

Close at hand, too, is the Big Sur Valley, situated just below the Andrew Molera park. The Big Sur Valley is in many ways the population center of the Big Sur Coast, and it has in it, located along the highway, the Big Sur Village, where there are three restaurants, two motels, the Ripplewood Resort — comprising a general store, delicatessen, service station and rental cabins — and two campgrounds, Big Sur and Riverside, both with tent sites, trailer hook-ups, and rental cabins. There are also some shops here, as well as a Grange Hall where the area's cultural events and town meetings are held.

Adjoining Big Sur Village to the southeast is the delightful, 810-acre Pfeiffer-Big Sur State Park, named for one of Big Sur's earliest settlers, John Pfeiffer. The park lies mainly to the east of the highway, with the Big Sur River winding through it, quite enchantingly. The park has over 200 campsites and trailer spaces and good picnicking and fishing possibilities. It also has many miles of hiking trails — including one that leads to the picturesque Pfeiffer Falls — as well as several short, guided walks, led by park rangers. At the entrance to the park is the Big Sur Lodge, featuring clusters of cabins in a wooded setting, a restaurant, swimming pool and sauna, a recreation room, a gift shop and grocery store. Also, near the southern end of the park is the Big Sur Station, which has in it the Big Sur Post Office and a U.S. Forest Service Office, from where you can obtain wilderness permits for the Ventana Wilderness and other parts of the Los Padres National Forest.

Of interest, too, at the southwestern end of the state park, is

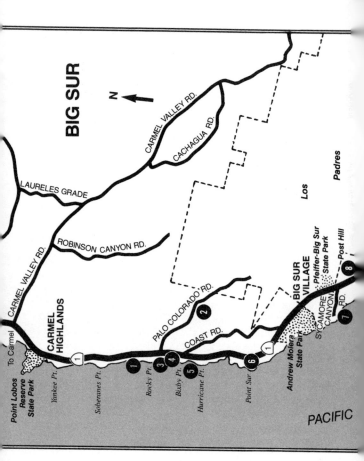

BIG SUR

N

CARMEL VALLEY RD.

CACHAGUA RD.

LAURELES GRADE

ROBINSON CANYON RD.

CARMEL VALLEY RD.

To Carmel

CARMEL HIGHLANDS

Point Lobos Reserve State Park

Yankee Pt.

Soberanes Pt.

Rocky Pt.

Bixby Pt.

Hurricane Pt.

Point Sur

PALO COLORADO RD.

COAST RD.

Andrew Molera State Park

BIG SUR VILLAGE

Pfeiffer-Big Sur State Park

Post Hill

SYCAMORE CANYON RD.

Los

Padres

PACIFIC

Points of Interest-
1) Garrapata Beach
2) Palo Colorado Canyon
3) Notley's Landing
4) Rocky Creek Bridge
5) Bixby Creek Bridge
6) Point Sur Lighthouse
7) Sycamore Canyon
8) Ventana
9) Nepenthe
10) Henry Miller Memorial Library
11) Deetjun's Big Sur Inn
12) Coast Gallery
13) Partington Ridge
14) Esalen Institute
15) Big Creek Bridge
16) Mission San Antonio de Padua
17) Hearst Castle

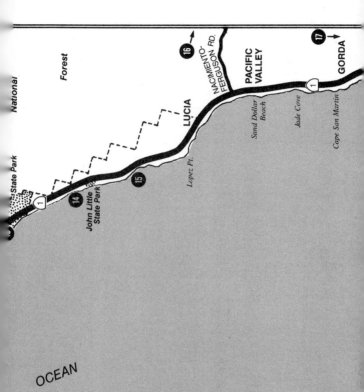

Sycamore Canyon, reached by way of the narrow, mountainou
Sycamore Canyon Road which goes off the highway, westward
The Sycamore Canyon Road leads — at its west end — t
Pfeiffer Beach, one of the most beautiful beaches on the Big Su
Coast, with a lagoon, several dramatic sea-carved rocks and rock
formations, windswept sand dunes, and tall sea cliffs. The beach
has good picnicking possibilities, although swimming is no
encouraged due to the strong undercurrents.

South from the Pfeiffer-Big Sur State Park, about a mile, is
Post Hill, an historical landmark in the area, originally home-
steaded in the late 1860s, and where, recently, archaeological
finds have been made, establishing a pre-Esselen Indian people
in the area more than 3,000 years ago. Close to Post Hill, also,
is the famous Ventana Resort, with its gourmet restaurant and
bar situated on a hill overlooking the ocean, and the luxurious
Ventana Country Inn located nearby, on a wooded hillside. There
is also a general store with a delicatessen here, as well as a
service station, located on a lower level, nearer the highway.

A half-mile or so below the Ventana Resort, on the west side
of the highway, is Nepenthe, a restaurant and bar-cum-gift shop,
originally built in 1944 as the honeymoon cottage of Orson
Welles and Rita Hayworth, designed by a student of Frank Lloyd
Wright, Rowan Maiden. Nepenthe — meaning "surcease from
sorrows" — sits on the edge of the rocky coast, more than 800
feet above the ocean, with unsurpassed, panoramic views of the
Pacific. There are, in fact, two restaurants here — one on the
upper deck, serving seafood and steaks, and the other, a cafe, on
the lower level, with an outdoor dining patio — as well as The
Phoenix gift shop, featuring souvenirs, postcards, books, jewelry, crafts and clothing. The gift shop and restaurants are open
daily.

Not far from Nepenthe is the Henry Miller Memorial Library,
with an excellent collection of books, letters, photographs and
other memorabilia of Henry Miller, one of Big Sur's most
famous writers and artists, who brought the area world renown.
The library is housed in the former home of Big Sur artist and
long-time associate of Henry Miller, Emil White. Library hours
are generally 10-7.

South still, quite close to Nepenthe and the Henry Miller
library, is Deetjun's Big Sur Inn, a Norwegian country-style inn,
with comfortable accommodations, a restaurant, and some
worthwhile nature trails; and south of there, another 2 miles or
so, at the end of Lafler Canyon, is the Coast Gallery, housed in
two large, redwood water tanks. The Coast Gallery has in it a
gift shop, with souvenirs, postcards and books of local interest,
as well as on-going exhibitions of art and sculpture, including a
superb display of original watercolors by Henry Miller. The
gallery is open daily during business hours.

The Carmel Mission, California's second oldest mission, dates from 1771

Old, Steinbeck-era buildings on Monterey's Cannery Row

Weathered old pier at Fisherman's Wharf, Monterey

Children dressed in Monarch butterfly costumes march in Pacific Grove's Butterfly Parade

Farther along, some 3 miles south of the Coast Gallery, off Highway 1, are Partington Ridge and Partington Cove, the former with its associations to writers Henry Miller and Lillian Bos Ross, who lived on the ridge at different times. At Partington Cove there is a 200-foot-long tunnel, dating from the 1800s, when the cove was a major shipping point for tanbark and timber harvested along the Big Sur Coast. Partington Cove was also an important supply point for the area before the completion of Highway 1.

Adjoining to the south of Partington Cove is the 1700-acre Julia Pfeiffer Burns State Park, with camping facilities and dozens of scenic walks, including one that leads to the magnificent Saddle Rock Falls, at the end of McWay Creek, claimed to be the only waterfalls on the California coast that plunge directly into the sea. The park also has picnicking possibilities, and is a good place to view sea otters. The park is named for Big Sur pioneer John Pfeiffer's sister, Julia.

Southward another 4 miles is the Esalen Institute, formerly a mineral hot springs resort, which offers, by reservation, residential workshops on psychology, philosophy and self-awareness; and immediately to the south of there lies the tiny John Little State Park, with few facilities, but with superb ocean views. Also of interest, 3 miles or so farther on, at the mouth of Big Creek, is the picture-perfect Big Creek Bridge, which is frequently mistaken for the Bixby Bridge by first-time visitors to the area. The Big Creek Bridge is 90 feet high and more than 500 feet long, and dates from 1937.

4 miles south of the Big Creek Bridge lies the small town of Lucia, named for Lucia Dani, the town's first postmistress. Lucia has a restaurant, a grocery store, a service station, and a lodge comprising a handful of rustic cabins, picturesquely perched above the Lucia Cove, all with expansive ocean views.

Farther still, some 2 or 3 miles from Lucia is the Kirk Creek Bridge, from the south end of which the wild, mountainous Nacimiento-Fergusson Road branches off Highway 1, eastward, journeying inland through several miles of unspoiled wilderness, then over the 4000-foot Nacimiento Summit to lead to Jolon, roughly 35 miles, and on to King City which is situated at the intersection of Highway 101, 55 miles distant. At Jolon, of course, you can visit the ancient Mission San Antonio de Padua, the third of California's 21 Spanish missions, established in 1771 by Franciscan Father Junipero Serra. There is a small museum at the mission, open to public viewing.

Returning to our main route of travel, however, approximately 4 miles south of the Kirk Creek Bridge on Highway 1 are the small community of Pacific Valley, with a gift shop, restaurant, grocery store and service station; the Sand Dollar Beach, which has picnic facilities; and Jade Cove, with its string

of coves streaked with jade, especially interesting to rock
hounds and jade collectors. Interestingly, at Jade Cove, in 1971,
a 9000-pound jade rock, more than 8 feet long and valued at
$180,000 — believed to be one of the largest such pieces of jade
ever found — was recovered from the ocean.

South of Jade Rock, the highway curves around Cape San
Martin — which has an automatic navigational light located
atop a rocky promontory — and on to Gorda, another small
community, with a cafe, grocery store and service station.
Gorda, which is the Spanish word for "fat," is named for an
oversized rock just offshore, said to resemble a fat lady. The
town was founded in 1932.

From Gorda it is roughly 26 miles south on the coastal
Highway 1 to San Simeon, the star attraction of the Central
Coast, which not only has good beaches but also one of California's great treasures — the Hearst Castle. The "castle" is indeed
a place not to be missed, visited by more than a million tourists
each year. It was originally the home of newspaper legend
William Randolph Hearst, and was built over a period of some
twenty years, 1922-1941, by noted San Francisco architect, Julia
Morgan. It comprises a magnificent, Spanish cathedral-style
main building and a handful of adjoining, and equally lovely,
mansions, all perched on a hill — in the Santa Lucia range —
overlooking the ocean. Within the castle you can view the
astonishing Hearst art collection, with countless rare and priceless treasures — among them rugs, tapestries, exquisite antique
furniture, and ornate, one-of-a-kind ceilings. On the grounds,
too, are beautiful gardens, with exotic trees and plants, and
lavish pools, both outdoor and indoor. The estate itself encompasses some 250,000 acres, mostly wild, rolling country, where
zebra, elk, goats and other wild animals once roamed free, in
what was then considered to be the largest private zoo in the
world. The estate was deeded to the state by the Hearst Corpo-
ration in 1958, and is now maintained by the State Parks Department, who conduct guided tours of the castle daily. There are
four tours offered, by which to see the castle, each covering a
different section of it, and reservations are advised, especially
for tours on weekends and holidays.

DETOURS

Salinas and South

East of Monterey on Highway 68, some 18 miles or so, lies
Salinas, situated at the heart of the fertile, north-south Salinas
Valley. Salinas is of course the seat of Monterey County, and an

mportant farming center, billed as "the nation's salad bowl." The city itself is surrounded by hundreds of acres of rich farmand, planted primarily with lettuce and celery, and at the center of it, also of interest, is the Salinas Old Town, the city's first shopping center, comprising some nine city blocks, where several historic buildings have been restored, and more than 200 businesses have located.

Salinas also has its associations with Nobel and Pulitzer prize-winning novelist John Steinbeck. Steinbeck, in fact, was born here, and many of his novels, such as *East of Eden*, *Of Mice and Men* and *Tortilla Flats*, draw heavily on his early experiences in the Salinas Valley. Steinbeck's former childhood home, a two-story Victorian, now restored and housing a restaurant, is located on Central Street in the Old Town, and can be visited during scheduled hours; it has some Steinbeck memorabilia, and a gift shop on the premises as well. Nearby, too, and well worth visiting, are the Steinbeck Library, located on West San Luis Street and housing some of Steinbeck's first editions, original manuscripts, letters, photographs and tapes; and the Harvey-Baker House, located on East Romie Lane, near Main Street, originally built as the home of Salinas' first mayor, Isaac Harvey, and now maintained as a living museum, with period furnishings, 19th-century fashions and other memorabilia.

Another place of interest, just on the outskirts of Salinas, at the corner of Boronda Road and West Laurel Drive, is the historic Boronda Adobe, one of the oldest buildings in the area, and the only remaining unmodified Mexican Rancho-era adobe. The adobe was originally built in 1848 as the home of Jose Eusebio Boronda, an early-day rancher, and is now a designated State Historical Landmark, preserved as a History Center, with exhibits of original furnishings, the Boronda family's personal possessions, and other artifacts depicting California's Mexican period. There is a small, one-room schoolhouse adjacent to the adobe, also of interest, dating, again, from 1848. Both the adobe and schoolhouse are open to public viewing.

South of Salinas, of course, some 23 miles on Highway 101, lies Soledad, where you can visit the site of Mission Nuestra Senora de Soledad, the thirteenth of California's 21 Spanish missions, founded in 1791 by Father Lasuen, and named for "Our Lady of Solitude." There is a modern chapel at the site of the mission now, which, nevertheless, incorporates in it — in its front wall — part of the original adobe wall of the old mission. The site of the mission can be reached by way of Arroyo Seco Road, west off the highway (101), then Fort Romie Road north a little way to the intersection of Mission Street; the chapel is located on Mission Street.

Worth visiting, too, roughly 10 miles northeastward on Highway 146, is the Pinnacles National Monument, which contains in it remnants of an ancient volcanic mountain, with spectacular spires and crags rising more than 1200 feet above the canyon floor. The park has several hiking trails meandering through it, leading to some extraordinary cave formations, canyons and peaks, with names like The Balconies, Machete Ridge, and High Peaks. There is also a visitor center here, and picnic areas and two campgrounds.

South of Soledad on Highway 1, another 20 miles or so, is King City, an agricultural center of sorts, where you can visit the Monterey County Agricultural and Rural Life Museum, located in the San Lorenzo County Park on Broadway. The museum has in it a restored farmhouse, barn, blacksmith shop, railroad depot and one-room schoolhouse; it also features several superb artifacts and displays, depicting the history of Monterey County agriculture, from the Indian-Mission period to present day. The park also has some recreational vehicle and camping facilities.

San Juan Bautista

Returning to Salinas, some 21 miles northeastward on Highways 101 and 156 is the sleepy little mission village of San Juan Bautista, the great glory of which is the historic Mission San Juan Buatista, the largest and most successful of California's 21 Spanish missions, founded in 1797 by Franciscan Father Lasuen. The mission is open to the public.

Also of interest, located adjacent to the mission, is the 6-acre San Juan Bautista State Historic Park, where several old, historic buildings and adobes from the Mexican and early American periods have been restored and furnished as living house museums, with 19th-century antiques and other artifacts, depicting life in California in the mid-1800s. Notable among these is the Plaza Hotel, originally built in 1858; the Zanetta House, also dating from 1858; and the Plaza Hall and Plaza Stable, the latter with displays of vintage carriages and wagons and a blacksmith shop. There are also 19th-century Spanish Gardens and other historical exhibits in the park, besides which it hosts several special events throughout the year, including "Living History Days" on weekends. The park is open to the public daily, 10-4.30.

Castroville and Moss Landing

Another nearby place of interest, 8 miles northeast of Salinas on Highways 183 and 1, is Castroville, famous as the "Artichoke Center of the World." The town, in fact, is surrounded, almost completely, by fields of artichokes — some 12,000 acres — producing more than 70 million pounds of the leafy green thistle, comprising roughly 90% of the nation's artichoke crop. In Castroville itself there are two or three fruit stands retailing, besides fresh produce, locally grown artichokes. The best known of these, located in the heart of town on Merritt Street, is The Giant Artichoke, quite possibly Castroville's foremost tourist attraction. It has at the front of it a giant artichoke sculpture, besides which there is also a deli-cum-restaurant here, offering a variety of artichoke foods, including steamed artichokes, marinated artichokes, deep-fried artichokes, artichoke soups, artichoke sandwiches and artichoke cup-cakes. A gift shop on the premises features artichoke souvenirs and "Giant Artichoke" T-shirts.

For artichoke lovers, Castroville also hosts an Artichoke Festival in September each year, when the first of the artichoke buds ripen. The festival attracts more than 25,000 visitors and features a wide variety of artichoke foods and festivities, and several events centered around the artichoke, including the crowning of "Miss Artichoke." Interestingly, in the late 1940s, we are told, Marilyn Monroe, then a fledging actress, came to Castroville to be crowned "Miss Artichoke."

Immediately north of Castroville, another 2 miles on the coastal Highway 1, is Moss Landing, with its tiny, historic harbor, dating from the 1870s. Moss Landing has one or two fruit stands and fish markets, and a handful of worthwhile seafood restaurants. There are also a dozen or so antique stores here, especially interesting to the first-time visitor, most of them nestled along Moss Landing Road which dashes off just to the back of the highway.

Moss Landing's great glory, however, is the Elkhorn Slough Bird Estuary, situated just inland from the sea, east off the highway on Elkhorn Road. The estuary comprises over 1300 acres of marshland and tidal flats — believed to be the second largest estuarine reserve in the country — and has hundreds of species of invertebrates, fish and birds, including a variety of hawks, falcons, vultures, shorebirds, waterfowl, gulls, pelicans, cormorants, egrets and heron. The reserve also has hiking trails, guided nature walks on weekends, and kayaking and canoeing possibilities.

Of interest, too, nearer the highway, west of Elkhorn Slough, is the PG&E steam power plant, originally built in 1948 and claimed to be the second largest plant of its kind in the world.

PRACTICAL INFORMATION FOR THE MONTEREY PENINSULA

HOW TO GET THERE

Monterey

Monterey is approximately 125 miles southeast of San Francisco, situated at the head of Monterey Bay. The best way to reach it is on the all-important *Highway 101* or *280* — with a brief detour southwestward on *Highways 156* and *1* or *68* and *1*.

Monterey also has a commercial airport, situated at the eastern edge of town, off Fremont Street. It is serviced by the following airlines: *United Airlines* (800) 241-6522; *US Air* (800) 428-4322; *Skywest* (800) 453-9417; *American Eagle* (800) 433-7300.

Pacific Grove

Pacific Grove adjoins immediately to the west of Monterey, and can be reached on any of several different interconnecting streets between the two towns, including *Ocean View Boulevard*, which is in fact a continuation of Monterey's well-known Cannery Row, and *Lighthouse Avenue*, which goes off Monterey's Hawthorne Street.

Pebble Beach

Pebble Beach lies directly south of Pacific Grove and Monterey. There are four gates by which to enter the area — two in Pacific Grove, on *17-Mile Drive* and *Sunset Drive*; one on *Highway 1*, some 3 miles south of Monterey's Fremont Street exit; and one at the southern end of the tract at Carmel, on *North San Antonio Avenue*. There is an admission fee of $6.00 charged for entry to Pebble Beach.

Carmel

Carmel is situated at the head of Carmel Bay, some 130 miles southeast of San Francisco, directly below Pebble Beach and the Monterey Peninsula. It can be reached either by way of Pebble Beach, or directly south on *Highway 1*, roughly 4 miles from Monterey.

Carmel Valley

The Carmel Valley lies just inland from Carmel, and can be reached by following *Highway 1* south from Monterey some 4 miles, then

Carmel Valley Road eastward directly into Carmel Valley.

Big Sur

Big Sur lies to the south of Carmel, stretching some 90 miles or so along the California Central Coast. The best way to reach it is by way of Carmel, directly south on the scenic coastal route, *Highway 1*. The Big Sur Village is approximately 25 miles from Carmel.

TOURIST INFORMATION

Monterey Chamber of Commerce and Visitor & Convention Bureau, 380 Alvarado St., Monterey; (408) 649-1770. Tourist literature, including accommodation and restaurant listings, calendar of events, Old Monterey maps, and several free tourist publications. Monterey also has a *Restaurant Hotline* for restaurant information and reservations; (408) 372-DINE.

Pacific Grove Chamber of Commerce, cnr. Central Ave. and Forest Ave., Pacific Grove; (408) 373-3304. Tourist brochures and listings of accommodations, restaurants, and places of interest; also "Butterfly Trees" map, and calendar of events.

Carmel Business Association. Cnr. San Carlos St. and 5th Ave., Carmel; (408) 624-2522. Carmel Gallery Guide and other tourist literature available. Also schedule of local events.

Carmel Valley Chamber of Commerce, 71 Carmel Valley Rd., Carmel Valley; (408) 659-4000. Tourist brochures and area maps; information on Carmel Valley wineries.

Salinas Chamber of Commerce, 119 E. Alisal St., Salinas; (408) 372-3214. Tourist literature, including listings of area accommodations and restaurants; also information on Steinbeck House and Steinbeck Library, and other area attractions. Calendar of events.

Big Sur Chamber of Commerce, P.O. Box 87, Big Sur, CA 93920; (408) 667-2100. Local map, and information on area accommodations, restaurants and shops.

ACCOMMODATIONS

Monterey

The Arbor Inn. *$59-$109.* 1058 Munras Ave.; (408) 372-3381. 56 rooms, some with fireplaces; also spa, phones, TV. Complimentary continental breakfast. Non-smoking rooms; handicapped facilities.

Bay Park Hotel. *$60-$110.* 1425 Munras Ave.; (408) 649-1020. Full-service hotel with 80 rooms. TV, phones; pool, jacuzzi, restaurant and cocktail lounge.

Best Western De Anza Inn. *$55-$95.* 2141 N. Fremont St.; (408) 646-8300/(800) 528-1234. 42 rooms; TV, phones. Heated pool. Handicapped facilities.

Best Western Monterey Inn. *$58-$118.* 825 Abrego St.; (408) 373-5345/(800) 528-1234. 79 rooms, with TV and phones; some fireplaces. Pool, hot tub.

Best Western Ramona Inn. *$54-$115.* 2332 Fremont St.; (408) 323- 2445/(800) 528-1234. 34 rooms with TV and phones. Restaurant and pool. Handicapped facilities.

Best Western Steinbeck Lodge. *$48-$109.* 1300 Munras Ave.; (408) 373-3203/(800) 528-1234. 32 rooms. TV, phones; pool.

California Motel. *$29-$109.* 2042 Fremont St.; (408) 372-5851. 47 rooms, including some with kitchens. TV, phones; pool and spa. Handicapped facilities.

Cannery Row Inn. *$65-$140.* 200 Foam St.; (408) 649-8580. 32 rooms, some fireplaces and balconies; some ocean view rooms; phones, TV, spa.

Carmel Hill Motor Lodge. *$40-$95.* 1374 Munras Ave.; (408) 373-3252. 38 rooms; TV, phones, and pool.

Casa Munras Garden Hotel. *$70-$350.* 700 Munras Ave.; (408) 375-2411. 150 rooms; phones, TV, some fireplaces. Also restaurant and heated pool.

Casa Verde Inn. *$45-$80.* 2113 N. Fremont; (408) 375-5407. 18 rooms, with TV and phones.

Colton Inn of Monterey. *$80-$180.* 707 Pacific St.; (408) 649-6500/(800) 848-7007. 48 rooms, many with fireplaces and in-room spas. TV, phones. Handicapped facilities.

Comfort Inn-Carmel Hill. *$48-$95.* 1252 Munras Ave.; (408) 372-2908/(800) 228-5150. 29 rooms with TV and phones. Pool; handicapped facilities.

Comfort Inn-Del Monte Beach. *$45-$130.* 2401 Del Monte Ave.; (408) 373-7100/(800) 228-5150. 47 rooms; TV and phones. Handicapped facilities.

Cypress Gardens Inn. *$49-$99.* 1150 Munras Ave.; (408) 373-2761/(800) 433-4732/(800) 422-4732 in California. 46 rooms with TV and phones. Pool, spa. Continental breakfast.

Cypress Tree Inn. *$52-$195.* 2227 Fremont St.; (408) 372-7586. 55 rooms, some with fireplaces; phones, TV. Hot tub and sauna.

Days Inn. *$50-$100.* 1400 Del Monte Ave., Seaside; (408) 394-5335/(800) 325-2525. 143 rooms, some with fireplaces. TV, phones, pool and spa. Also restaurant on premises.

Del Monte Pines. *$50-$125.* 1298 Munras Ave.; (408) 375-2323. 19 rooms with TV and phones. Heated pool.

Doubletree Hotel. *$120-$175.* 2 Portola Plaza; (408) 649-4511. One of Monterey's largest luxury hotels, with 374 well-appointed rooms. Tennis courts, pool, spa; gourmet restaurant.

El Adobe Inn. *$50-$80.* 936 Munras Ave.; (408) 372-5409/(800) 433-4732/(800) 422-4732 in California. 24 rooms with TV and phones. Hot tub. Continental breakfast.

El Castell Motel. *$32-$90.* 2102 Fremont St.; (408) 372-8176. 48 units with TV and phones; heated pool.

Franciscan Inn. *$40-$95.* 2058 Fremont St.; (408) 375-9511. 47 units, some with kitchens. TV, phones; pool, hot tub.

Holiday Inn Express-Cannery Row. *$85-$145.* 443 Wave St.; (408) 372-1800. 43 rooms with TV and phones. Hot tub. Continental breakfast. Located one block from the beach.

Holiday Inn Resort of Monterey. *$100-$175.* 1000 Aguajito Rd.; (408) 373-6141. 203-room resort hotel. Facilities for guests include a swimming pool, spa, tennis courts, restaurant and cocktail lounge.

Hotel Pacific. *$145-$265.* 300 Pacific St.; (408) 373-5700. Luxury hotel with 104 rooms, most with fireplaces; also spa.

Hyatt Regency. *$135-$200.* 1 Old Golf Course Rd.; (408) 372-1234. 579-room resort hotel, with tennis courts, golf course, pool, hot tub and sauna; also gourmet restaurant and cocktail lounge. Many of the rooms have fireplaces.

Lone Oak Motel. *$38-$80.* 2221 Fremont St.; (408) 372-4924. 45 rooms, some with fireplaces. TV, phones, spa. Handicapped facilities.

Mariposa Inn. *$68-$165.* 1386 Munras Ave.; (408) 649-1414. 51 rooms, some with fireplaces. TV, phones, pool, hot tub. Handicapped facilities.

Monterey Bay Inn. *$120-$350.* 242 Cannery Row; (408) 373-6242/(800) 424-6242. 47 rooms with private balconies; spectacular bay views. Also health club on premises, and hot tub, sauna, and special wash-down facilities for scuba divers. Complimentary continental breakfast.

Monterey Beach Hotel. *$89-$169.* 2600 Sand Dunes Dr.; (408) 394-3321. 196-room beachfront hotel, with pool, hot tub, and restaurant.

Monterey Downtown Travelodge. *$50-$100.* 675 Munras Ave.; (408) 373-1876/(800) 255-3050. 49 units with TV and phones. Heated pool, and tennis court.

Monterey Fairgrounds Travelodge. *$48-$90.* 2030 N. Fremont St.; (408) 373-3381/(800) 255-3050. 104 units; TV, phones. Restaurant and cocktail lounge. Heated pool.

The Monterey Hotel. *$110-$185.* 406 Alvarado St.; (408) 375-3184. 45 rooms, some with fireplaces. TV and phones. Continental breakfast.

Monterey Motor Lodge. *$55-$110.* 55 Camino Aguajito; (408) 375-3184. 45 rooms with TV and phones. Snack bar; heated pool. Continental breakfast.

Monterey Pines. *$50-$150.* 1288 Munras Ave.; (408) 375-2168. 34 units, with TV and phones; some units with spa and fireplace. Hot tub; continental breakfast.

The Monterey Plaza. *$150-$280.* 400 Cannery Row; (408) 646-1700. 290 guest rooms, with ocean and bay views. The hotel also has a restaurant and cocktail lounge on the premises.

Monterey Marriott Hotel. *$120-$170.* Cnr. Del Monte Ave. and Calle Principal; (408) 649-4234. 5-star hotel, with 344 rooms; pool, sauna, fitness center, restaurant and cocktail lounge. Handicapped facilities.

Montero Lodge. *$40-$70.* 1240 Munras Ave.; (408) 375-6002. 20 units; TV and phones. Continental breakfast.

Munras Lodge. *$45-$200.* 1010 Munras Ave.; (408) 646-9696. 29 units, some with fireplaces and in-room spas; TV, phones. Continental breakfast.

Otter Inn. *$75-$190.* 571 Wave St.; (408) 375- 2299. 31 rooms, with TV and phones; some fireplaces. Hot tub. Handicapped facilities. Continental breakfast, served in room.

Padre Oaks Motel. *$55-$110.* 1278 Munras Ave.; (408) 373-3741. 20 units with TV and phones. Pool. Continental breakfast.

Pelican Inn. *$50-$120.* 1182 Cass St.; (408) 375-2679. 19 units, some with fireplaces. TV and phones; outdoor pool.

San Carlos Inn. *$65-$120.* 850 Abrego St.; (408) 649-6332/(800) 227-6332. 55 units, some with fireplaces. TV, phones; hot tub, and tennis court. Handicapped facilities. Continental breakfast.

Sand Dollar Inn. *$60-$125.* 755 Abrego St.; (408) 372-7551/(800) 982-1986. 63 rooms, some with fireplaces. TV, phones; pool.

Spindrift Inn. *$150-$490.* 652 Cannery Row; (408) 646-8900. 42 rooms, with fireplaces, down comforters and feather beds. TV and phones. Hot tub. Continental breakfast, served in bed.

Vagabond Motel. *$32-$110.* 2120 Fremont St.; (408) 372-6066. 19 units, some kitchenettes. TV and phones.

Victorian Inn. *$119-$299.* 487 Foam St.; (408) 373-8000/(800) 225- 2902/(800) 232-4141 in California. 68 rooms, some with fireplaces; TV, phones, hot tub.

Way Station Inn. *$60-$120.* 1200 Olmsted Rd.; (408) 372-2945. 46 rooms, with TV and phones. Fireplaces in some rooms; also restaurant on premises. Handicapped facilities.

West Wind Lodge. *$50-$120.* 1046 Munras Ave.; (408) 373-1337. 53 rooms, some with fireplaces and kitchens; some in-room jacuzzis. TV and phones. Indoor pool and spa. Continental breakfast.

Pacific Grove

Andril Fireplace Cottages. *$65-$95.* 569 Asilomar Blvd.; (408) 375-0994. 18 self-contained cottages with fireplaces and kitchens. Hot tub.

Beachcomber Inn. *$55-$150.* 1996 Sunset Dr.; (408) 373-4769. 26 units, with TV and phones. Pool, sauna, and restaurant. Complimentary continental breakfast. Bicycles available for guests' use.

Bide-A-Wee Motel. *$50-$90.* 221 Asilomar Blvd.; (408) 372-2330. 17 units, with TV. Some family units with kitchens.

Butterfly Grove Inn. *$50-$100.* 1073 Lighthouse Ave.; (408) 373-4921. 28 units, some with kitchens and fireplaces. TV and phones; heated pool and spa.

Best Western Butterfly Trees Lodge. *$60-109.* 1150 Lighthouse Ave.; (408) 372-0503. 68 units; heated pool, hot tub and sauna. Continental breakfast; wine and cheese in the evening.

Executive Lodge. *$60-$150.* 660 Dennett Ave.; (408) 373-8777/(800) 221-9323. 30 condominium units, with full kitchens, fireplaces, private decks and garages. TV, phones. Handicapped facilities.

Larchwood Inn. *$50-$75.* 740 Crocker Ave.; (408) 373-1114. 38 units; TV and phones. Some fireplaces, kitchens, and balconies.

Lighthouse Lodge. *$79-$200* 1249 Lighthouse Ave.; (408) 655-2111/(800) 858-1249. 98 rooms and suites with TV and phones, some with fireplaces, jacuzzis and microwaves. Heated swimming pool, spa. Complimentary breakfast, and evening wine and hors d'oeuvres.

Pacific Gardens Inn. *$70-$150.* 701 Asilomar Blvd.; (408) 646-9414. 28 units, with TV, phones, and fireplaces. Hot tub. Continental breakfast.

Pacific Grove Motel. *$40-$90.* Cnr. Lighthouse Ave. and Grove Acre Ave.; (408) 372-3218. 30 units; TV, phones, refrigerators. Pool and hot tub. Barbecue area.

Pacific Grove Quality Inn. *$80-130.* 1111 Lighthouse Ave.; (408) 646-8885/(800) 228-5151. 49 rooms and suites with TV and phones. Some units with fireplaces and kitchens. Pool, sauna, jacuzzi. Handicapped facilities. Complimentary continental breakfast.

Rosedale Inn. *$105-$185.* 775 Asilomar Blvd.; (408) 665-1000/(800) 822-5606 in California. 18 units, with TV, phones, and wet bars; some units with jacuzzi tubs, fireplaces, and kitchenettes. Spa and sun deck. Continental breakfast.

Sea Breeze Motel. *$45-$65.* 1100 Lighthouse Ave.; (408)372-7775. 36 units; TV and phones. Some cottages and suites with kitchens.

Sunset Motel. *$45-$85.* 133 Asilomar Blvd.; (408) 375-3936. 20 units, some with kitchens and fireplaces. TV. Continental breakfast.

Terrace Oaks Inn. *$48-$75.* 1095 Lighthouse Ave.; (408) 373-4382. 11 rooms; TV, phones. Complimentary continental breakfast.

Wilkies Motel. *$45-$75.* 1038 Lighthouse Ave.; (408) 372-5960/(800) 439-4553. 24 units with TV and phones, some with kitchens; also some ocean view units. Continental breakfast.

Pebble Beach

The Lodge at Pebble Beach. *$280-$1500.* 17-Mile Drive, Pebble Beach; (408) 624-3811/(800) 654-9300. Luxury resort, located at the world-famous Pebble Beach Golf Course. 161 well-appointed rooms, with phones, TV, wet bar and refrigerators; some fireplaces, and views. The Lodge also features 4 superb restaurants, a beach, heated pool and sauna, 13 tennis courts, and jogging and horseback riding facilities.

The Inn at Spanish Bay. *$230-$1200.* 17-Mile Drive, Pebble Beach; (408) 647-7500/(800) 654-9300. Newly-built 270-room luxury resort, with two restaurants, shops and boutiques, tennis courts, and an 18-hole championship golf course.

Carmel

Adobe Inn. *$120-$210.* Dolores St. and 8th; (408) 624-3933. 20 rooms; TV, phones, pool, hot tub, restaurant and cocktail lounge. Some rooms with ocean views and fireplaces. handicapped facilities.

Best Western Carmel Bay View Inn. *$79-120.* Junipero St., between 5th Ave. and 6th Ave.; (408) 624-1831/(800) 528-1234. 68 rooms; TV, phones. Pool.

Candle Light Inn. *$85-$130.* San Carlos St. and 5th Ave.; (408) 624-6451/(800) 433-4732. 19 rooms, some with fireplaces and ocean views; TV, phones, pool and restaurant. Complimentary continental breakfast.

Carmel Fireplace Inn. *$75-$150.* San Carlos St. and 4th Ave.; (408) 624-4862/(800) 634-1300 in California. 18 rooms, patio units, cottages and suites, some with fireplaces; also TV, refrigerators, and in-room coffee. Beautiful gardens.

Carmel Mission Inn. *$89-$150.* Hwy. 1 and Rio Rd.; (408) 624-1841/(800) 348-9090. 165 units; TV, phones, pool, and hot tub. Restaurant on premises features live entertainment.

Carmel Oaks Inn. *$90-$125.* Mission and 5th Ave.; (408) 624-5547. 17 rooms, some with ocean views; TV, phones. Complimentary continental breakfast. Handicapped facilities.

Carmel Resort Lodge. *$90-$140.* Carpenter St. and 2nd Ave.; (408) 624-3113. 26 units; TV, phones, spa.

Carmel River Inn. *$40-$80.* Hwy. 1 at the Carmel Bridge; (408) 624-1575. 43 rooms; TV, phones, pool.

Carmel Studio Lodge. *$75-$150.* Junipero St. and 5th Ave.; (408) 624-8515. 19 units, with TV and phones; some kitchens. Also heated pool

Carmel Torres Inn. *$80-$125.* Ocean Ave. at Torres St.; (408) 624-3387. 17 units, including some with ocean views. TV, phones, pool

Carmel Townhouse Lodge. *$65-$145.* San Carlos St. and 5th Ave.; (408) 624-1261/(800) 528-1234. 28 units; TV, phones, and pool.

Carriage House Inn. *$135-$225.* Junipero St. between 7th Ave. and 8th Ave.; (408) 625-2585/(800) 433-4732. 13 units, some with fireplaces and ocean views. TV, phones; complimentary continental breakfast.

Coachman's Inn. *$65-$145.* 7th Ave. and San Carlos St.; (408) 624-6421/(800) 336-6421. 30 units; TV, phones; some kitchens.

Cypress Inn. *$80-$190.* 7th Ave. and Lincoln St.; (408) 624-3871/(800) 443-7443. 33 units; TV, phones. Some units with fireplaces and ocean views. Complimentary continental breakfast.

Dolphin Inn. *$70-$175.* San Carlos St. and 4th Ave.; (408) 624-5356/(800) 433-4732. 27 rooms, some with fireplaces and kitchens. TV and phones. Complimentary continental breakfast.

Highlands Inn. *$225-$650.* 4 miles south of Carmel on Hwy. 1; (408) 624-3801/(800) 682-4811. Large, remodeled resort hotel, situated above the spectacular Big Sur coast. 146 units, including 43 rooms with fireplaces and decks, and 103 suites with kitchen, living room, bedroom, spa, fireplace and ocean-view deck. Two restaurants on premises; also large outdoor pool and hot tub.

Hofsas House. *$75-$130.* San Carlos St. and 4th Ave.; (408) 624-2745/(800) 221-2548. 38 rooms, some with ocean views and fireplaces; TV, phones, pool, hot tub. Continental breakfast.

Horizon Inn. *$95-$155.* Junipero St. and 3rd Ave.; (408) 624-5327. 20 units with TV and phones; some fireplaces, balconies and ocean views. Pool. Continental breakfast.

Lamplighter Inn. *$70-$130.* Ocean Ave. at Camino Real; (408) 624-7372. 9 rooms, some with fireplaces; TV.

La Playa Hotel. *$110-$200.* Camino Real and 8th Ave.; (408) 624-6476/(800) 582-8900 in California. 3-story Spanish-style hotel, located two blocks from Carmel Beach. 75 units, featuring handcrafted furniture. Pool, gazebo, restaurant.

Lobos Lodge. *$90-$160.* Ocean Ave. and Monte Verde St.; (408) 624-3874. 27 units, with fireplaces, TV and phones. Continental breakfast.

Mission Ranch Resort. *$75-$175.* 26720 Dolores St.; (408) 624-6436. 25 units. TV, phones, restaurant and cocktail lounge. Continental breakfast. Handicapped facilities.

Normandy Inn. *$125-$199.* Ocean Ave. and Monte Verde St.; (408) 624-3825/(800) 343-3825 in California. 48 rooms, cottages, suites, and apartments; some kitchens, and fireplaces; TV, phones, pool. Continen-al breakfast.

Ocean View Lodge. *$90-$175.* Junipero St. and 3rd Ave.; (408) 524-7723. 8 rooms, some with fireplaces and ocean views; TV, phones. Continental breakfast.

The Pine Inn. *$90-$190.* Ocean Ave., between Lincoln and Monte Verde Sts.; (408) 624-3851/(800) 228-3851. Century-old inn, with 49 rooms. TV, phones, restaurant and cocktail lounge.

Sundial Lodge. *$95-$165.* Monte Verde St. and 7th Ave.; (408) 624-8578. 19 units, some with kitchens; TV, phones, continental breakfast.

Svensgaards Inn. *$70-$185.* San Carlos St. and 4th Ave.; (408) 624-1511/(800) 433-4732. 34 units with TV and phones, some fireplaces. Pool. Continental breakfast.

Tally Ho Inn. *$95-$250.* Monte Verde St. and 6th Ave.; (408) 624-2232. 14 units, some with fireplaces; also TV, and phones.

Tickle Pink Inn. *$140-$260.* 155 Highland Dr.; (408) 624-1244/(800) 635-4774. 35 rooms, some with fireplaces and ocean views; TV and phones. Hot tub.

Tradewinds Inn. *$69-$125.* Mission St. and 3rd Ave.; (408) 624-2776/(800) 624-6665. 27 units; TV, phones, pool. Some ocean view units. Continental breakfast.

Wayside Inn. *$70-$195.* Mission St. and 7th Ave.; (408) 625-5336/(800) 433-4732. 21 units, some with fireplaces. TV, phones. Continental breakfast.

Carmel Valley

Blue Sky Lodge. *$50-$85.* Flight Rd. and Poppy Rd.; (408) 659-2256. 15 units with TV and phones; some fireplaces, and kitchens. Pool and hot tub.

Carmel Valley Inn. *$55-$120.* Carmel Valley Rd. and Los Laurelos; (408) 659-3131. 46 units, TV and phones. Tennis courts, swimming pool, hot tub; also restaurant.

Carmel Valley Ranch Resort. *$200-$650.* Old Ranch Rd.; (408) 625-9500. 100 rooms with TV, phones, fireplaces and jacuzzis. Also swimming pool, hot tub, tennis courts, 18-hole championship golf course. Restaurant on premises. Handicapped facilities.

Los Laureles Lodge. *$75-$400.* W. Carmel Valley Rd.; (408) 659-2233. 30 rooms and suites, with TV, phones, fireplaces, jacuzzis and kitchens. Swimming pool, hot tub, restaurant.

Quail Lodge. *$145-$275.* 8205 Valley Greens Dr.; (408) 624-1581/(800) 583-9516/(800) 682-9303 in California. 100 luxury units, many with fireplaces. The lodge also offers golf and tennis facilities, and a pool, spa and restaurant.

Stonepine. *$195-$575.* 150 E. Carmel Valley Rd.; (408) 659-2245. Secluded hide-away; 12 units with fireplaces, TV and phones. Pool, spa; day transportation and airport transfers for hotel guests.

Big Sur

Big Sur Campground and Cabins. *$65-$95.* Hwy. 1, Big Sur; (408) 667-2322. 8 units, including 3 wooden A-frames and 5 modular cabins. Fireplaces, some with kitchens; picnic and barbecue facilities.

Big Sur Lodge. *$90-$135.* Pfeiffer-Big Sur State Park, Big Sur; (408) 667-2171. 61 cottages, some with kitchens and fireplaces. Heated pool, restaurant, grocery store.

Deetjen's Big Sur Inn. *$45-$135.* Hwy. 1, Big Sur; (408) 667-2377. Rustic 19 room-inn, built in the 1930s and set amid the redwoods. Restaurant on premises.

Fernwood Resort. *$50.* Hwy. 1, Big Sur; (408) 667-2422. 12 units. Grocery store, restaurant and bar.

Glen Oaks Motel. *$60-$75.* Hwy. 1, Big Sur; (408) 667-2105. 14-unit adobe motel in garden setting. Restaurants nearby.

Lucia Lodge. *$55-$95.* Hwy. 1, Lucia; (408) 667-2391. 10 cottages in clifftop setting, with spectacular ocean views. Restaurant, gas station and small store.

Ripplewood Resort. *$40-$75.* Hwy. 1, Big Sur; (408) 667-2242. 16 cabins, some with kitchens, some with fireplaces. Situated along the Big Sur river. Breakfast cafe, grocery store, and restaurant across the street.

River Inn Resort. *$55-$140.* Hwy. 1, Big Sur; (408) 625-5255/(408) 667-2237. 20 units, some with kitchens. Heated pool, restaurant and bar.

Ventana Inn. *$155-$775.* Hwy. 1, Big Sur; (408) 624-4812. 59-unit luxury inn. TV, phones, fireplaces. Pools, hot tub, restaurant and cocktail lounge.

Post Ranch Inn. *$290-$450.* Hwy. 1, Big Sur; (408) 986-7080. Newly-built, unique oceanfront luxury inn, featuring hand-hewn wood and hand-cut stonework. 30 units, some with sod roofs, some on stilts among redwood groves, and most with panoramic ocean views. Dining room on premises.

San Simeon

Best Western Cavalier. *$70-$100.* 9415 Hearst Dr., San Simeon; (805) 927-4688/(800) 528-1234. Oceanside motel with 61 rooms with fireplaces and terraces. Heated pool, restaurant, cocktail lounge and bar.

Best Western Green Tree Inn. *$65-$90.* Hwy. 1, San Simeon; (805) 927-4691/(800) 528-1234. 118 rooms with TV and phones. Heated indoor pool, game room, and tennis courts.

Carriage Inn. *$60-$80.* 9280 Castillo Dr., San Simeon; (805) 927-8659/(800) 556-0400. 48 units, some with private decks and ocean views. Spa.

El Rey Inn. *$55-$80.* Hwy. 1, San Simeon; (805) 927-3998. 56 units, some with whirlpool spas. Heated pool. Continental breakfast.

Sands Motel. *$40-$60.* 9355 Hearst Dr., San Simeon; (805) 927-3243. 33 units with TV and phones. Heated indoor pool. Continental breakfast.

Silver Surf Motel. *$29-$75.* 9390 Castillo Dr., San Simeon; (805) 927-4661. 72 units; TV and phones. Some units with fireplaces and ocean views. Indoor heated pool, jacuzzi, sundeck.

Salinas

Appling Inn. *$40-$65.* 1030 Fairview Ave., Salinas; (408) 422-6486. 44 rooms and suites with TV, phones and wet bars.

Best Western Airport Motor Inn. *$45-$75.* 555 Airport Blvd., alinas; (408) 424-1741/(800) 528-1234. 96 rooms with phones and TV. ome rooms with jacuzzis. Heated pool, and spa. Continental breakfast. enny's restaurant adjacent.

El Dorado Motel. *$45-$60.* 1351 N. Main, Salinas; (408) 449-442/(800) 523-6506. 44 rooms, with TV and phones; some with fireaces. Hot tub. Non-smoking rooms.

Laurel Inn. *$58-$80.* 801 Laurel Dr., Salinas; (408) 449-2474/(800) 54-9831. 145 rooms with TV and phones; some suites with fireplaces. eated pool, hot tub and sauna. Restaurant and cocktail lounge adjacent. on-smoking rooms available.

Ramada Inn. *$59-$125.* 808 N. Main St., Salinas; (408) 424-661/(800) 272-6232. 163 rooms and suites, all with TV and phone. eated pool. Restaurant and cocktail lounge with live entertainment.

BED & BREAKFAST INNS

Monterey

Del Monte Beach Inn. *$40-$75.* 1110 Del Monte Ave.; (408) 649-410. 18-room inn, housed in former boarding house for cannery work-rs, dating from 1925. Continental breakfast, comprising freshly-baked roissants, muffins and pastries, and fresh fruit and juices. No smoking.

The Jabberwock. *$90-$165.* 598 Laine St.; (408) 372-4777. Formerly a Dominican convent, the inn now offers 5 unique guest rooms. Spectacular ocean views from the third floor; milk and cookies by the fireplace in the living room in the evening.

Old Monterey Inn. *$165-$220.* 500 Martha St.; (408) 375-8284. English country house with beautiful gardens and oak trees. 10 rooms, ll with private baths; some fireplaces, skylights, and stained glass windows. Full breakfast, served in bed, in the dining room, or on the atio. Also picnic baskets for guests, provided upon request.

The Merritt House. *$120-$205.* 386 Pacific St.; (408) 646-9686. comfortable suites in historic adobe main house; 22 other rooms, ocated in newer buildings behind the main house. All rooms have rivate baths, fireplaces, phones and TVs, and are furnished with ntiques and brass beds. Beautiful rose garden on premises. Continen-al breakfast.

Pacific Grove

Centrella Hotel. *$85-$180.* 612 Central Ave.; (408) 372-3372. Award-winning Victorian inn, with 26 beautifully decorated rooms, including some attic suites and cottages; private baths, phones, TV, fireplaces. Continental breakfast; complimentary wine and sherry.

Gosby House Inn. *$85-$130.* 643 Lighthouse Ave.; (408) 375-1287. Turreted Victorian mansion; 22 rooms, 13 with fireplaces. Breakfast comprises homemade muffins, granola parfaits, fresh fruit and eggs; hors d'oeurves in the afternoon.

Martine Inn. *$115-$225.* 255 Ocean View Blvd.; (408) 373-3388 Elegant Victorian home, dating from 1899. 19 antique-filled rooms private baths with clawfoot tubs and marble sinks; phones, fireplaces hot tub. Spectacular bay views from front parlor.

The Old St. Angela Inn. *$95-$150.* 321 Central Ave.; (408) 372-3246. Historic country home, built in 1910. 8 delightful rooms, decorated with pine antiques; some private baths. Solarium overlooking English garden. Afternoon wine and cheese; champagne breakfast. No children; no smoking.

Seven Gables Inn. *$95-$185.* 555 Ocean View Blvd.; (408) 372-4341. 100-year-old Victorian mansion, located at the edge of Monterey Bay. 14 rooms with private baths; high tea; ocean views. No smoking.

Green Gables Inn. *$100-$160.* 104 5th St.; (408) 375-2095. Charming Queen Anne Victorian with carriage house, built in 1888. 10 guest rooms, most with fireplaces; some private baths. Antique furnishing quilts, fresh flowers. Full buffet-style breakfast, served in the dining room overlooking Monterey Bay. Afternoon wine and hors d'oeuvres No smoking.

Rosebox Country Inn by-the-Sea. *$125-$205.* 557 Ocean View Blvd.; (408) 373-7673. Oceanfront Victorian inn built in 1904. 8 individually-decorated rooms, each with ocean view. Fireplaces, down comforters. Full country breakfast, served in bed or in the morning room Evening wine and cheese.

Carmel

Cobblestone Inn. *$95-$175.* 8th Ave. and Junipero St.; (408) 625-5222 Newer bed and breakfast inn with 24 beautifully furnished rooms; private baths, fireplaces, TV and phones. Afternoon tea; continental breakfast.

Green Lantern Inn. *$60-$125.* Casanova St. and 7th Ave.; (408) 624-4392. 19 remodeled rooms and cottages in 1926 inn. Private baths some fireplaces. Garden setting; ocean views.

Happy Landing Inn. *$90-$145.* Monte Verde St. and 6th Ave. (408) 624-7917. 7 comfortable rooms, with fireplaces and TV. Continental breakfast.

Monte Verde Inn. *$85-$145.* Monte Verde St. and Ocean Ave. (408) 624-604/(800) 328-7707. Delightful old inn with 10 rooms; some ocean views, some fireplaces; private baths, TV. Continental breakfast.

Sandpiper Inn At The Beach. *$90-$165.* 2408 Bay View Ave. (408) 624-6433/(800) 633-6433 in California. 1930s inn, filled with antiques and fresh flowers, close to Carmel Bay. 15 rooms with private baths; some fireplaces. Complimentary sherry, continental breakfast.

Sea View Inn. *$80-$110.* Camino Real and 11th Ave.; (408) 624-8778. Bed and breakfast inn with 8 rooms. Continental breakfast, afternoon tea and wine and cheese.

Stonehouse Inn. *$90-$140.* Monte Verde St. and 8th Ave.; (408) 624-4569. 8 well-appointed rooms; hot tub. Wine and cheese in the evening.

Carmel Valley

Valley Lodge. *$99-$229.* Carmel Valley Rd. and Ford St., Carmel Valley; (408) 659-2261/(800) 641-4646. 31-room inn, featuring fireplaces

Ivy-covered shops in Carmel's famous shopping district

Casa Soberanes, a typical Monterey-style adobe, in the Monterey
State Historic Park

n some of the rooms. Phones, TV, pool and hot tub; continental break-
ast.

SEASONAL EVENTS

January

First Weekend. *Ben Hogan Pebble Beach Pro-Am Golf Tournament.* Held at the Spyglass Hill and Poppy Hills golf courses. Scheduled
for the first week of the month. For more information, call (408)
649-8500. The *Monterey Bay Symphony* features a series of concerts,
with performances in Monterey, Carmel and Salinas, throughout January, February, March, April and May. For information and schedule, call
(408) 372-6276.

February

First Weekend. *AT&T Pebble Beach National Pro-Am Golf Tournament.* Held at the Spyglass Hill, Poppy Hill and Pebble Beach golf
courses. Popular event, attracting more than 100,000 fans and partici-
pants. Features famous professional players, among them Arnold Pal-
mer, Jack Nicklaus and Lee Trevino. More information on (800)
541-9091.
Fourth Weekend. *Monterey Hot Air Affair.* Hot-air ballooning competition, held at Laguna Seca Raceway. Features over 40 balloons. For
more information and schedule of events, call (408) 649-6544.

March

First Weekend. *Colton Hall Birthday Celebration.* Annual open-
house at Colton Hall. Variety of festivities. (408) 375-9944. *Dixieland
Monterey.* Several nationally- and internationally-known jazz bands
perform at various locations throughout downtown Monterey. For locations and information on performers, call (408) 443-5260.
Third Weekend. *Monterey Wine Festival.* At the Monterey Conference Center. 3-day festival, with more than 200 California wineries
participating. Wine-tasting, wine seminars. Phone (800) 525-3378.

April

First Weekend. *Good Old Days Celebration.* Held in Pacific Grove.
Events include a parade, arts and crafts show, melodrama at California's
First Theatre, and a pie-eating competition. Phone (408) 373-3304 for
complete schedule of events. *Toyota Grand Prix.* At Laguna Seca Raceway. Prestigious motorcycle race, featuring world-class riders. (408)
648-5111.

Third Weekend. *Victorian Home Tour.* Pacific Grove. Tour of several of Pacific Grove's famous Victorian homes; popular annual event. For tour reservations, call (408) 373-3304. *Wildflower Show.* Held at the Pacific Grove Museum of Natural History. The show features one of the finest exhibits of wildflowers in California. (408) 648-3116/373-3304.

Fourth Weekend. *Monterey Adobe Tour.* Downtown Monterey Tours of 25 of Monterey's historic adobes; annual event. Reservations on (408) 372-2608. *Big Sur International Marathon.* At Big Sur, Hwy. 1. More than 2,000 marathon runners from around the country compete in this event. Marathon begins at Pfeiffer Big Sur State Park, leading north along the coast to Carmel. (408) 625-6226.

May

Second Weekend. *Salinas Valley Fair.* At the Salinas Valley Fairgrounds in King City. 5-day event, includes a rodeo, carnival rides, agricultural exhibits and demonstrations, and an arts and crafts show. (408) 385-3243.

Fourth Weekend. *The Great Monterey Squid Festival.* Monterey County Fairgrounds; (408) 649-6544. Food, music, live entertainment, arts and crafts booths; squid prepared dozens of different ways.

June

Second Weekend. *Outdoor Summer Art Festival.* Sunset Center, Carmel. Over 100 artists, sculptors and craftspeople from Monterey County exhibit and sell their work. (408) 659-5099.

Third Weekend. *Monterey Bay Blues Festival.* At the Monterey Fairgrounds, Monterey. Well-known national and regional blues musicians perform; also soul food. For information and reservations, call (408) 394-2652.

Fourth Weekend. *Forest Theater.* Cnr. Mountain View Ave. and Santa Rita St., Carmel. Regular performances of Shakespeare, as well as repertory theater and musicals. Season runs from June through October. For program information and reservations, contact the theater at (408) 655-7529/626-1681.

Fourth Weekend. *California State Amateur Golf Championship.* Hosted by Pebble Beach, Spyglass Hill, Cypress Point, Del Monte and Carmel Valley Golf & Country Club courses. The tournament is now in its 77th year. For more information, call (408) 649-8500/625-4653.

July

First Weekend. *Fourth of July Celebration.* Events include a birthday party at Colton Hall, with music, live entertainment, food concessions and carnival games, followed by a fireworks display over Monterey Bay. Call (408) 646-3866 for more information.

Second Weekend. *Carmel Bach Festival.* Usually held in mid-July, at the Sunset Center in downtown Carmel, with special performances at

he Carmel Mission. Renowned three-week-long festival; features recit-
ls and classical music concerts, offered by world-famous musicians.
lso lectures, symposia and a children's concert. Advance reservations
equired; (408) 624-1521. *IMSA Races.* Laguna Seca Raceway, Mon-
erey. Road car racing, featuring prototype race cars and stock cars.
408) 648-5111.

Third Weekend. *California Rodeo.* Salinas Rodeo Grounds, Sali-
las. One of the biggest rodeos in the State. Features bareback riding,
rick riding, roping, bucking bulls, and horse races; also cow milking
ompetitions. More information on (408) 757-2951.

Fourth Weekend. *National Horse Show.* At the Monterey County
airgrounds, Monterey. Well-established event, featuring show jump-
ng, dressage and other equestrian events. For a schedule and more
nformation, call (408) 372-1000.

August

First Weekend. *Scottish Festival and Highland Games.* At the
Monterey County Fairgrounds, Monterey. Colorful event, celebrating
Scottish heritage, with highland dancing, bagpipe music and athletic
competitions, including hammer throwing and tossing the caber. Also
Scottish food and crafts. (408) 394-1129/899-3864. *Encore California
International Musicfest.* A series of chamber music recitals, lectures and
concerts featuring works of 19th and 20th century composers. Call (408)
649-6544 for complete schedule. *Steinbeck Festival.* Salinas. City-wide
celebration, featuring a Steinbeck film festival and walking tours of the
Steinbeck House, the burial site of Steinbeck, and other historic sites,
buildings and adobes. Also readings and lectures centered around the
life and works of John Steinbeck. For a schedule of events, call (408)
758-7314.

Second Weekend. *Monterey County Fair.* Monterey County Fairgrounds, Monterey. Carnival, live entertainment, agricultural exhibits,
wine show. More information on (408) 372-5863.

Third Weekend. *Annual Pebble Beach Concours d'Elegance and
Christie's Auction.* Held at The Lodge at Pebble Beach. Antique car
show, with more than 100 American and European classic cars on
display; also auction. (408) 625-8562. *Annual Monterey Historic Auto-
mobile Races.* At Laguna Seca Raceway, Fort Ord. Vintage car races,
featuring over 150 restored automobiles of different vintages. Call the
raceway for more information; (408) 648-5111.

September

First Weekend. *Carmel Shakespeare Festival.* Long-standing event
which takes place at Forest Theater, Carmel. Local and professional
actors perform; also children's matinee. Call (408) 649-0340/655-3200
for tickets and schedule. *Coastweeks.* Statewide, 3-week-long event
dedicated to the appreciation and preservation of California's bays,
beaches, and estuaries. Activities include Coastal Cleanup Day, kite
flying competition and nature walks. Call (800) 262-7848 for schedule
of events in the Monterey area. *Greek Festival.* This annual event

features Greek food, music, dancing and traditional crafts. More information on (408) 424-4434.

Second Weekend. *Santa Rosalia Festival.* Custom House Plaza, Old Monterey. Traditional Italian festival. Events include a parade, blessing of the fleet, and outdoor mass; also food concessions and live entertainment. Phone (408) 626-2050.

Third Weekend. *Monterey Jazz Festival.* Monterey County Fairgrounds. Popular 3-day Jazz Festival, featuring such greats as Count Basie, Joe Williams, Art Blakey and Clark Terry. Also concerts by California High School All-Star Jazz Band. Advance reservations suggested; (408) 373-3366. *Castroville Artichoke Festival.* Castroville Celebration of Castroville's artichoke harvest. Features a large variety of gourmet artichoke foods, artichoke eating contest, a parade, arts and crafts show and live entertainment. More information on (408) 633-CHOK.

Fourth Weekend. *Fiesta de San Carlos Borromeo.* Held at the Carmel Mission in Carmel. Annual event, featuring ethnic food, arts and crafts show, mariachi bands and dancing. Call (408) 624-1271 for more information. *Sandcastle Contest.* At the Carmel Beach. Popular annual event with over 400 entrants creating elaborate sand structures, including profiles, castles and cars. Hosted by the American Institute of Architects. For exact dates and more information, call (408) 624-2781. *California International Air Show.* Salinas Airport, Salinas. One of the largest air shows in the State, held in late September or early October. Features air races, hot-air ballooning competition, and aerobatic exhibitions. Live entertainment, food concessions. (408) 754-1983.

October

First Weekend. *Oktoberfest.* At the Monterey County Fairgrounds, Monterey. Traditional German festival, with German food, beer, and music. (408) 649-6544.

Second Weekend. *Butterfly Parade.* In Pacific Grove. Colorful parade through downtown Pacific Grove, celebrating the annual Monarch butterfly migration; creative costumes, local school bands. (408) 373-3304. *California Constitution Day Celebration.* Held on October 13th, at Colton Hall in Monterey. Festivities and celebrations commemorating the drafting of California's first constitution in Monterey in 1849. Includes a re-enactment of the historic event. (408) 646-3851. *Old Monterey Heritage Festival.* Over 100 local Monterey artists display and sell their work; also historical displays, live entertainment, gourmet food. Call (408) 373-3720 for additional information.

November

Second Weekend. *Robert Louis Stevenson's Un-birthday.* At the Stevenson House in Monterey; scheduled for November 13th. The town of Monterey celebrates the birthday that Robert Louis Stevenson legally gave away to a child born on Christmas Day. Docents in period costumes conduct tours of the house in which Robert Louis Stevenson once ved. For more information, call (408) 649-7118.

Third Weekend. *Home Crafters Marketplace.* In Carmel, 300 local rtists and craftspeople exhibit a wide variety of artwork. (408) 659-5099.

December

First Weekend. *Festival of Trees.* Held at the Monterey County Fairgrounds. Display of trees decorated with unique, handcrafted ornaments. Miniature art auction, entertainment, and country store. More information on (408) 372-5477. *Christmas at the Inns.* Pacific Grove. Tours of several of Pacific Grove's Victorian bed and breakfast inns, all of which are decorated for the Christmas season. More information on (408) 373-3304.

Second Weekend. *Christmas in the Adobes.* Downtown Monterey. Features public tours of many of Monterey's historic adobes, including some tours at night. Adobes are decorated for the holidays. (408) 649-7118.

PLACES OF INTEREST

Monterey

Monterey Bay Aquarium. Located at the west end of Cannery Row. This is one of the largest aquariums in the country, and the chief attraction of Monterey, visited by an estimated 2.5 million tourists each year. The aquarium features a variety of superb marine exhibits, including a 90-foot-long recreation of a cross-section of Monterey Bay; a giant *kelp forest*, claimed to be the tallest aquarium exhibit in the United States, rising two full stories and containing 350,000 gallons of sea water; and the *Marine Mammal Gallery*, which has life-sized displays of whales and other marine mammals. There are also several tidal and petting pools for children, and a large *Shorebird Aviary*. Vast decks with panoramic views of Monterey Bay; also gift and book shop on premises. Admission fee: $9.75 adults, $7.25 seniors and students, $4.50 children. Open daily 10-6 (except Christmas). For reservations and information, call (408) 375-3333.

Cannery Row. Historic, mile-long street, immortalized by John Steinbeck in his book of the same name, *Cannery Row.* The "row," which stretches from the Coast Guard Station in the east to the Monterey Bay Aquarium in the west, running along the bay, is lined with colorful old sardine canneries. During the early 1900s, there were some 19 canneries situated along here, processing in excess of 235,000 tons of sardines annually. Most of the canneries closed in 1951, and several were destroyed by fire in the following years. The surviving canneries are now being restored and converted into fashionable little arcades, featuring fine shops and boutiques, restaurants and art galleries. For more information on Cannery Row, call the *Cannery Row Association* at (408) 373-1902.

Spirit of Monterey Wax Museum. 700 Cannery Row; (408) 37?-
3770. Housed in the old Monterey Canning Company building, th
museum features life-sized wax exhibits of over 100 famous Canner
Row characters, among them the eccentric marine biologist "Doc
Rickett, and Sam Mally, Hazel, Mac and Lee Chong. Also wax model
of other historical characters and scenes, including the building of th
Monterey mission. Open daily 9 a.m.-9 p.m. Admission fee: $4.9
adults, $3.95 students and seniors, $2.95 children (under 6 free).

Allen Knight Maritime Museum. 550 Calle Principal; (408) 375
2553. Nautical museum, housing an extensive collection of maritim
artifacts, including hundreds of photographs, prints and paintings o
ships, old steering wheels, compasses, bells, lanterns, navigation instru
ments, ship name-boards, naval history books, old shipping records—
including a number of volumes of the old Lloyd's Register—and, mos
impressive of all, the original Fresnel Light from the Point Sur Light
house, dating from 1880. Also on display are scale models of Sebastia
Vizcaino's ship, *San Diego*, and Commodore Sloat's flagship, *Savan
nah*. Museum hours: 1-4 Tues.-Fri., 2-4 Sat.- Sun. No admission fee
donations accepted.

Monterey Peninsula Museum of Art. 559 Pacific St.; (408) 372
5477. Permanent exhibits of folk art, paintings, sculpture and graphics
Also regularly changing exhibits, as well as special exhibits of early-day
Monterey area artists. Open 10-4 Tues.-Sat., 1-4 Sun.; closed Mondays
and holidays.

Fisherman's Wharf. Colorful old wharf, with three or four seafooc
restaurants, specialty and gift shops, and fish markets. Stroll the weathered piers, and watch sea lions and pelicans. Also, sportfishing charters
and whale-watching cruises are available from here. Nearby, at the
Municipal Wharf you can watch fishing boats unload their catch of the
day. The Municipal pier is also a good place for pier fishing.

Dennis the Menace Playground. Situated at the El Estero Lake
Park, just off Pearl Street. Beautifully landscaped park, designed by
Hank Ketchum, creator of "Dennis the Menace"; features imaginative
mazes, slides and tunnels, and a stationary steam locomotive. Variety of
play equipment, boat rentals, and picnic areas.

Also see **Monterey Path of History**.

Pacific Grove

Lover's Point Park. Located along Ocean View Blvd., near Pacific
Ave. Scenic, 32-acre oceanfront park, with a secluded crescent-shaped
beach, offering spectacular views and swimming possibilities. Also
picnic areas and restrooms, walking paths, and bird-watching.

Asilomar State Beach. Located at the west end of Pacific Grove.
State beach, with a 105-acre beach-front conference center, comprising
303 guest rooms, 48 meeting rooms, a heated swimming pool and
nearby facilities for volleyball, golf and tennis. The beach itself has
some tidepools, and picnicking and surfing possibilities.

Butterfly Trees Park. Between Melrose and Alder Sts., at the west
end of town. Comprises part of the 22-acre George Washington Park —
located along the Alder Street side of it — named for its "Butterfly
Trees" where Pacific Grove's famous orange-black Monarch butterflies

winter each year, Oct.-Mar., hanging in giant clusters, like dried leaves, from the trees. The park has some picnic areas.

Museum of Natural History. Cnr. Central and Forest Aves.; (408) 648-3116 One of the best small museums of its kind in the country. Features displays of over 400 species of birds native to Monterey County, as well as exhibits depicting the animal, plant and mineral life of the Monterey Peninsula. Also on display are a superb relief map of Monterey Bay, illustrating the great chasm in the bay, and rotating exhibits of Native American artifacts. Museum hours are 10-5, Tues.-Sun.

Point Pinos Reserve. Situated along the northwest tip of Pacific Grove, between Ocean View Blvd. and Asilomar Ave. Small coastal reserve, with an operating lighthouse, built in 1855 and claimed to be the oldest continuously operating lighthouse on the West Coast—with the original Fresnel lenses and prisms still in use. There is also a small museum housed in the lighthouse building, devoted entirely to Coast Guard history. The lighthouse is open for self-guided tours on weekends, 1-4. For more information, call (408) 648-3116.

Pacific Grove Art Center. Lighthouse Ave.; (408) 375-2208. The center comprises 4 art galleries and 18 artists' studios, in a Victorian setting. Features year-round exhibitions of paintings, sculpture, graphic art and photographs. Also offers workshops, lectures and concerts. Open 12-5 Tues.-Sat., 1-4 Sun. Free admission; donations accepted.

American Tin Cannery. 125 Ocean View Blvd. (just west of the Monterey Bay Aquarium). Formerly housing the American Can Company, a manufacturing facility for sardine cans during the 1930s and 1940s. Now a shopping mall, with an assortment of fine shops and boutiques, factory outlet stores, and restaurants.

Pebble Beach

Spanish Bay. Situated at the northern end of Pebble Beach, approximately one mile south of Pacific Grove. Lovely, crescent-shaped bay, with a resort of the same name, comprising a 270-room luxury hotel, and an 18-hole golf course with a clubhouse, several shops and boutiques, and two restaurants. The bay is named for Monterey's founder, Gaspar de Portola's landing here in 1769. Resort phone, (408) 647-7500/(800) 654-9300.

Point Joe. Located just to the south of Spanish Bay, comprising a land mass jutting out into the ocean, frequently mistaken by sailors in the early days to be the entrance to Monterey Bay, resulting in several shipwrecks just offshore. Just off Point Joe, too, is the "Restless Sea," one of the few places in the world where ocean currents meet, creating unusual turbulence.

Bird and Seal Rocks. 4 miles south of Spanish Bay, comprising two rocky outcroppings just offshore, where countless seagulls, black cormorants and other shoreline birds can be seen in their natural habitats, as well as herds of sea lions, sea otters and the smaller leopard and harbor seals. Picnic area located along the shore, overlooking the Bird and Seal rocks.

Fanshell Beach. Crescent-shaped white-sand beach, just south of Bird and Seal rocks. Superb views. Picnic area.

Cypress Point. Located at the southern tip of Pebble Beach, with lookout that offers unobstructed views of the Pebble Beach coastline t the north and Carmel Bay and the northern portion of the Big Sur Coas to the south. Quite close to Cypress Point is the *Cypress Point Gol Course,* built in 1928 and ranked among the top 20 courses in the U.S. especially notable for its 16th green, which can only be reached b driving over some 200 yards of open ocean.

Crocker Grove. 13-acre reserve, adjoining to the south of the Cy press Point Golf Course. Contains some of the largest and oldest Mon terey Cypress on the peninsula.

The Lone Cypress. $1\frac{1}{2}$ miles east of Cypress Point. This is one o Monterey Peninsula's most famous landmarks and its most photo graphed sights, comprising a lone cypress tree, clinging to virtually bare rock, overlooking the ocean.

Ghost and Witch Trees. At Pescardero Point, a mile east of the Lone Cypress. The Ghost and Witch trees are two dramatic Monterey Cypress, with trunks bleached white by the wind and sea spray, de scribed by Robert Louis Stevenson as "ghosts fleeing before the wind."

The Lodge at Pebble Beach. 1 mile north of Pescadero Point, at the head of Stillwater Cove. Oceanfront resort, the oldest and best-known in the area, dating from 1919. Offers luxury guest accommodations, restaurants, several fine shops, tennis courts, an equestrian center, and a world-class, 18-hole golf course with oceanfront greens and fairways.

Carmel

Carmel Mission. Located on Rio Rd., off Hwy. 1.; (408) 624-3600. Second oldest of California's 21 Spanish missions, originally founded by Father Junipero Serra in Monterey in 1770, and moved to its present site, overlooking the Carmel River, in 1771. Mission museum features some excellent exhibits, including the original altar brought across by Father Serra from Baja California. Also view crypt inside mission, where Fathers Serra, Lasuen and Crespi are buried. Gift shop on prem ises. Open Mon.-Sat. 9.30-4.30; Sun. 10.30-4.30. Donations accepted.

Tor House. Located at Carmel Point, between Stewart Way and Ocean View Ave., just south of Carmel Village. Picturesque, granite stone house overlooking Carmel Bay, built by California poet Robinson Jeffers, between 1918-1930, as his home. Features a spectacular 40-foot tower—the Hawk Tower—which contains stones taken from the Great Wall of China, Pyramid of Cheops and Hadrian's Villa. Also view secret staircase in tower, and an ancient porthole between the second and third floors, reputed to have come from the ship on which Napoleon escaped from Elba in 1815. Tours of the house (for small groups only) are conducted on Fridays and Saturdays, 10-3; admission fee: $5.00. For reservations, call (408) 624-1840.

Carmel Beach. Picture-perfect beach, with white sand and crashing surf, framed by gnarled Monterey Cypress. The beach is open to the public for picnicking and ocean walks; swimming is discouraged due to shifting currents.

Point Lobos Reserve. 1 mile south of the Carmel River Bridge on Hwy. 1; (408) 624-4909. 1,250-acre state-owned coastal reserve, with sea lion and sea otter colonies and brown pelican breeding grounds. The

eserve is also a good place for whale watching—in season. Picnic
acilities available; also hiking trails. Open daily 9-5 (9-7 in summer);
dmission fee: $6.00 per car.

Carmel Valley

The Barnyard. Unique shopping complex with some 55 specialty
nd import shops, art galleries, bakeries and restaurants — including the
Thunderbird Bookshop and Cafe — housed in nine beautifully restored
barns. Lavish flower gardens.

Korean Buddhist Temple. On Robinson Canyon Rd., south of
Carmel Valley Rd; (408) 624-3686. Oriental, wood-frame temple, situated on a wooded, $7\frac{1}{2}$-acre site, overlooking Carmel River. The temple
s open to the public during Sunday services.

Garland Ranch Regional Park. Located near the intersection of
Carmel Valley Rd. and Los Laureles Grade; (408) 659-4488. 3,600-acre
park, with picnicking, fishing, horseback riding and bird-watching possibilities, and more than 7 miles of nature trails. Trail maps available at
the visitor center, located just inside the park.

Big Sur

Garrapata State Park. Located at Soberanes Point, just off Hwy. 1,
approximately 8 miles south of Carmel. Superb headlands with all-
around views, and a lovely, curved beach, reached by way of a path
leading down from the highway. Also view the Garrapata Creek Bridge,
just to the south, with a span of 150 feet.

Bixby Bridge. Located on Hwy. 1, at Bixby Creek, some 13 miles
south of Carmel. One of the most photographed sights on the Big Sur
coastline. Bridge dates from 1932, claimed to be the longest concrete
arch span bridge in the world at the time of its construction, with a
central span of 320 feet and a height of 260 feet. Observation alcoves
located along the bridge at intervals, with good views of Bixby Creek
Canyon and the ocean.

Point Sur State Historic Park. 6 miles south of Bixby Bridge, off
Hwy. 1. Comprises 350-foot-high volcanic rock, just offshore, with an
historic lighthouse at the top of it. The lighthouse dates from 1889, and
is still in operation. Limited public access, with guided tours on Sat. (10
a.m. and 2 p.m.) and Sun. (10 a.m.). Call for tour reservations; (408)
625-4419.

Andrew Molera State Park. 2,154-acre scenic nature reserve, situated 8 miles south of Bixby Bridge, lying largely between Hwy. 1 and
the coastline. Includes 4 miles of coastline, with a mile-long sandy
beach. Also offers hiking, picnicking fishing and horseback riding possibilities, and a primitive campground. Park phone: (408) 667-2315.

Pfeiffer-Big Sur State Park. Located near Big Sur Village, approximately 13 miles south of Bixby Bridge, off Hwy. 1. 821-acre wooded
park, named for John Pfeiffer, an early settler. Hiking trails, guided
nature walks in summer, picnic facilities, and a campground with 200
campsites. Also in the park are a lodge and restaurant. Day-use fee:
$6.00. Park phone, (408) 667-2315; lodge phone, (408) 667-2171.

Nepenthe. Hwy. 1, 2 miles south of Big Sur Village. Popular cliff top restaurant, with sweeping views of the Big Sur coastline. Nepenthe—which means "surcease from sorrows"—was originally built in 1944 as the honeymoon cottage of Orson Welles and Rita Hayworth, designed by a student of Frank Lloyd Wright, Rowan Maiden. Now houses a restaurant on its upper deck, and a cafe and outdoor patio on the lower level. Also gift shop on premises, selling souvenirs, postcards, books, jewelry, crafts and clothing. Restaurant phone, (408)-667-2345; gift shop phone, (408) 667-2347.

Henry Miller Memorial Library. Located on Hwy. 1, just south of Nepenthe. Contains a excellent collection of books, letters, photographs, and other memorabilia of author-painter Henry Miller, one of Big Sur's most famous residents. Open Tues.-Sun. 11-5; free admission. (408) 667-2574.

Coast Gallery. 3½ miles south of Nepenthe on Hwy. 1, at the mouth of Lafler Canyon. This rustic gallery, housed in huge redwood water tanks, features the work of local artists and sculptors, and also an extensive exhibit of Henry Miller paintings and lithographs. On summer weekends local artists can be seen at work. Gift shop on premises. Open daily 9-5:30. Phone, (408) 667-2301.

Julia Pfeiffer Burns State Park. 1,700-acre day-use park, sprawled on both sides of the highway, some 9 miles south of Big Sur Village. Facilities include picnic areas and restrooms, and several hiking trails, including a nature walk along redwood-lined McWay Creek, passing through a tunnel, to McWay Cove, where you can view the magnificent Saddle Rock Falls, claimed to be the only waterfall on the California coast which plunges directly into the ocean. Park phone, (408) 667-2315. Day use fee, $6.00.

Esalen Institute. On Hwy. 1, 13 miles south of Big Sur Village. New Age retreat; offers workshops on exploring human potential through psychology, mind and body philosophies and self- awareness exercises. Hot spring baths; massage facilities. Limited public access. For reservations and more information, call (408) 667-3000.

Mission San Antonio de Padua. Located 30 miles east of Hwy. 1 (5 miles west of Jolon); follow Nacimiento-Fergusson Rd. off Hwy. 1, then Mission Rd. directly to the mission. This is the third of California's 21 Spanish missions, founded in 1771 by Father Junipero Serra. Features a chapel, courtyard garden, and a small museum with displays of mission artifacts. Open to public viewing Mon.-Sat. 10-4.30, Sun. 11-5; Mission phone, (408) 385-4478.

Hearst Castle. 125 miles south of Monterey on Hwy. 1, at San Simeon. Spectacular, multi-level Spanish-cathedral-style "castle," perched on a hill overlooking the ocean; formerly home of newspaper legend William Randolph Hearst. Now owned and operated by the State Parks Department, the castle houses the fabulous Hearst art collection, featuring priceless paintings, sculptures, antiques, period furniture, rare tapestries and rugs, and several handcrafted, one-of-a-kind ceilings. Also featured here are superb, landscaped grounds, with exotic trees and plants, and lavish indoor and outdoor pools. The estate itself comprises approximately 250,000 acres of rolling coastal land in the Central Coast's Santa Lucia Range, where once buffalo, zebra, elk, exotic deer and other animals roamed free, in what was described as the largest private zoo in the world. Castle originally built between 1922 and 1941,

designed by architect Julia Morgan. There are four different tours of the
castle and grounds, conducted by park personnel, each covering a different section of the estate. For tour information and reservations, call
(800) 446-PARK.

Salinas

Salinas Old Town. Salinas' original shopping district, comprising
nine city blocks in the center of downtown Salinas, housing more than
200 businesses. The Steinbeck Library and Steinbeck's house are part
of the Old Town, together with several other historic buildings.

Steinbeck House. 132 Central Ave.; (408) 424-2735. Two-story
Victorian, formerly the childhood home of Pulitzer Prize-winning nov-
elist John Steinbeck, author of *Cannery Row, Sweet Thursday* and
Grapes of Wrath, among others. Now housing a restaurant and gift shop.
Steinbeck House is open to the public Mon.-Fri. 9-3; the restaurant is
open for lunch daily.

Steinbeck Library. 110 W. San Luis St., near Capitol St.; (408)
758-7311. Public library, housing an extensive collection of Nobel and
Pulitzer prize-winning author John Steinbeck's books — including several first editions — and personal correspondence and other memorabilia. Open Mon.-Thurs. 10-9, Fri.-Sat. 10-6.

Harvey-Baker House. 238 E. Romie Ln., near Main St. Victorian-
era house, originally built in 1868 as the home of Salinas' first mayor,
Isaac Harvey. Now owned and operated by the Monterey County Historical Society as a living museum, featuring period furnishings and
decor, 19th-century fashions, and other memorabilia. Open Sunday, 1-4,
or by appointment. (408) 424-7155.

Boronda History Center. Cnr. Boronda Rd. and W. Laurel Dr. One
of the oldest buildings in the area, and the only remaining unmodified
Mexican Rancho-era adobe, originally built in 1848 as the home of Jose
Eusebio Boronda, an early settler and rancher. The adobe is now a
designated State Historical Landmark, preserved as a History Center,
with exhibits of original furnishings, the Boronda family's personal
possessions, and other artifacts depicting California's Mexican period.
There is also a small, one-room schoolhouse here, dating, again, from
1848. Both the adobe and schoolhouse are open to the public, Mon.-Fri.,
9-3. For more information, call (408) 757-8085.

Pinnacles National Monument. Located 35 miles southeast of Salinas, with two entrances — one on Hwy. 146, 8 miles east of Soledad,
the other on Hwy. 25, 32 miles south of Hollister. The park contains
remnants of an ancient volcanic mountain, with spectacular spires and
crags rising to more than 1,200 feet above the canyon floors. Offers
several hiking trails, leading to extraordinary cave formations, canyons
and peaks, with names such as The Balconies, Machete Ridge, and High
Peaks. Picnic and barbecue areas, two campgrounds, and visitor center.
Park fee: $3.00 per car. Visitor center open daily 9-5. For more informa-
tion, call the park office at (408) 389-4485.

Monterey County Agricultural and Rural Life Museum. 1160
Broadway, King City; (408) 385-1484. Located in the San Lorenzo
County Park. Comprises a restored farmhouse, barn, blacksmith shop
and one-room schoolhouse. Displays of century-old farm equipment and

other artifacts depicting the history of agriculture in the area, from the mission-era to present day. Open daily 10-5.

San Juan Bautista

Mission San Juan Bautista. Located at the corner of San Juan Rd. and Hwy. 156, 3½ miles off Hwy. 101 (21 miles north of Salinas). This is one of the largest and most successful of California's 21 Franciscan missions, founded in 1797 by Father Lasuen. The mission is open to the public, 9.30-4.30 daily. Mission phone, (408) 623-4528.

San Juan Bautista State Historic Park. 6-acre historic park, comprising largely the old mission village of San Juan Bautista, located 21 miles north of Salinas, on Hwy. 156 and San Juan Rd. Tour the town's many historic buildings and adobes, mostly dating from the mid-1800s, and now largely restored and preserved as living museums, with original Mexican and early American period furnishings and artifacts. Also view 19th-century Spanish Gardens, and other historical exhibits. "Living History" weekends scheduled here on the first Saturday of each month. Open Wed.-Sun. 10-4.30. Park phone, (408) 623-4881.

Moss Landing

Elkhorn Slough. 1700 Elkhorn Rd., just east of Moss Landing. 1,330-acre estuary, believed to be the second largest of its kind in the country. Comprises marshlands, tidal flats, and tidal creeks, where hundreds of species of invertebrates, fish, and birds are to be found, including a variety of hawks, falcons, vultures, shorebirds, waterfowl, gulls, pelicans, cormorants, egrets and heron. The reserve also has hiking trails, guided nature walks on weekends, and kayaking and canoeing possibilities. Visitors center on premises, located at the main entrance, containing exhibits and a small bookstore. Hours: 9-5, Wed.-Sun.; day-use fee: $2.50/adults, children under 16 free. For more information, call (408) 728-2822.

MONTEREY PATH OF HISTORY

Custom House. Located at 1 Custom House Plaza, adjacent to Fisherman's Wharf. Picturesque old adobe, built in the early 1800s and claimed to be the oldest government building on the West Coast. Originally used as a toll-house during the Mexican era, to levy and collect taxes on goods brought in by merchant ships. In 1846, it was the site of the landing of Commodore John Drake Sloat, and where Sloat first raised the American flag and claimed Monterey and the rest of California for the United States. The Custom House now houses a small museum with displays of a typical cargo of a 19th-century merchant ship, such as dry goods, china, lanterns, cartwheels, pick-axes and shovels, and the like. The museum is open 10-4 daily.

Pacific House. Located directly behind the Custom House, on the Custom House Plaza. Splendid, two-story Monterey- style adobe, dating from 1847. Originally housed military offices, then a tavern-cum-ballroom. Now houses a museum, with several excellent exhibits of local historical interest, representing all four eras of Monterey's history — Indian, Spanish, Mexican and early American — displayed in a series of rooms, arranged by theme and period. Also of interest is the Spanish-style courtyard-garden at the back of the adobe, with age-old shade trees and seasonal flowers. Museum hours are 10-4 daily; admission fee: $2.00.

Casa Del Oro. Also at the Custom House Plaza, at the corner of Oliver and Scott Sts. Small, two-story Mexican era adobe, built around 1845 by Thomas Larkin, a wealthy merchant and first U.S. Consul to California. Once housed a general store—the old Joseph Boston Store— and also a gold depository. Now a gift shop of sorts, featuring Monterey souvenirs, gifts and postcards, books of local historical interest, and herbs from the tiny herb garden located adjacent to the store. Hours: Wed.-Sat. 10-4, Sun. 12-5.

California's First Theater. Cnr. Scott and Pacific Sts. Wood-frame and adobe structure, built in 1846 by Jack Swan, a seafaring Scotsman, as a lodging house and tavern for sailors. In 1850, the New York Volunteers first began staging plays here. Both the theater and tavern are still in operation, open to the public, with theater groups scheduling weekly performances, featuring 19th-century melodrama and comedy. Open daily during summer, 11.30-5 Sun.-Tues., 11.30-8 Wed.-Sat.; plays begin at 8 p.m.

Old Whaling Station. Between Pacific St. and the Custom House Plaza. Beautifully-restored two-story adobe, built in 1847 as the residence of David Wight, a Scotsman who modeled it on the plan of his ancestral home in Scotland, featuring a central hall. In 1855, the Old Monterey Whaling Company acquired the building and housed in it its offices and workers' quarters. Features a lovely balcony and garden, and a front walkway made, reportedly, from whale vertebrae. The building is generally open to the public on Tuesdays, 10-12.

First Brick House. Located next to the Old Whaling Station, between Pacific and Oliver Sts. Old, two-story brick building, dating from 1847 and believed to be the first structure in Monterey to be built entirely from bricks. Not open to the public, but may be viewed from outside.

Casa Soberanes. 336 Pacific St. Splendid old Monterey-colonial adobe, built in the 1840s and now restored to its former glory, with superb, well-kept gardens. Former home of the Soberanes family, from 1860 until 1922. Features early New England furnishings, China trade items, and Mexican folk art; also local artwork on display. Tours on the hour, 10-3 daily (except Thurs.); tour fee: $2.00.

Merritt House. On Pacific St., between Franklin and Del Monte Sts. Restored, two-story adobe, dating from the 1830s, formerly the residence of Josiah Merritt, Monterey County's first judge. The Merritt House is now privately owned.

Casa Serrano. Located on Pacific St., near Franklin St. Charming, single-story adobe, built largely in 1845, and now fully restored, with antique furnishings and decor. Home to several generations of the old Serrano family; now houses the Monterey History and Art Association offices. Open to public viewing, Sat.-Sun. 2-4.

Casa de Alvarado. Cnr. Jefferson and Dutra Sts. Restored, east-fac-

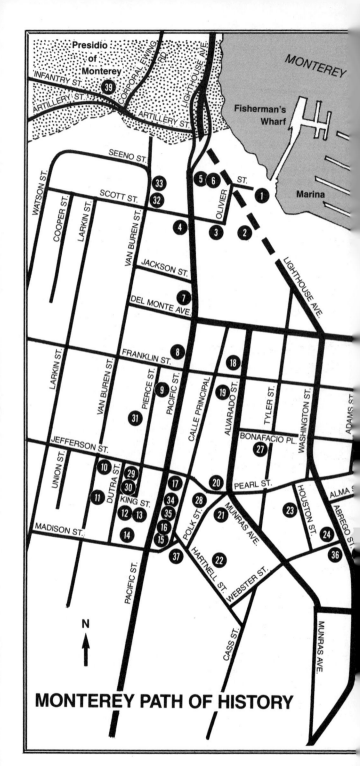

MONTEREY PATH OF HISTORY

N
↑

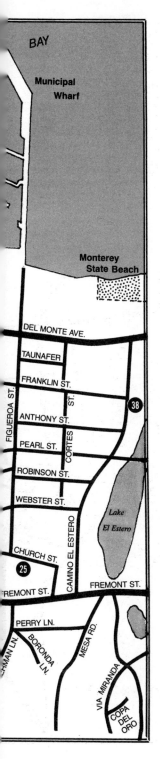

Points of Interest-
1) Custom House
2) Pacific House
3) Casa Del Oro
4) California's First Theater
5) Old Whaling Station
6) First Brick House
7) Casa Soberanes
8) Merritt House
9) Casa Serrano
10) Casa de Alvarado
11) Vasquez Adobe
12) Colton Hall
13) Old Monterey Jail
14) Underwood-Brown Adobe
15) Gutierrez Adobe
16) Miller Adobe
17) Larkin House
18) Rodriguez-Osio Adobe
19) Sanchez Adobe
20) Alvarado Adobe
21) Cooper-Molera Adobe
22) Fremont Headquarters
23) Stevenson House
24) Casa Abrego
25) Royal Presidio Chapel
26) Madriaga Adobe
27) Estrada Adobe
28) Casa Amesti
29) Casa De La Torre
30) Gordon House
31) Casa de Soto
32) Doud House
33) Mayo Hayes O'Donnell Library
34) Sherman-Halleck Adobe
35) House of Four Winds
36) Casa Pacheco
37) Stokes Adobe
38) French Consulate
39) The Presidio of Monterey

ing adobe, built in the 1830s by Juan Bautista Alvarado, first Monterey born governor of California. Features 24-inch-thick walls, and a roo fastened with thongs. The adobe is now preserved as part of the Mon terey State Historic Park.

Vasquez Adobe. On Dutra St., behind Colton Hall. Originally a single-story adobe, built in the early 1800s, home to Robin Hood-style bandit, Tiburcio Vasquez, as a child. The second floor, featuring a balcony, was added in later years by Louis Hill, of the well-known railroad family. The adobe now houses the City of Monterey offices.

Colton Hall. Pacific St., between Jefferson and Madison Sts. Elegant, two-story white-stone building, regarded as Monterey's most distinguished historic building, and also one of the city's oldest buildings of the American period. Originally built as a school in 1848 by Walter Colton, Monterey's first mayor and newspaper publisher, Colton Hall was the site of California's first Constitutional Convention in 1849. It now houses the City of Monterey offices on the first floor, and a museum on the second floor, devoted to Monterey history and the Constitutional Convention, with the original assembly hall, where the constitution was drafted, now restored and open to the public. Museum hours: 10-5 daily.

Old Monterey Jail. Located on Pacific St., adjacent to Colton Hall. Small, 6-cell jail, built in 1854 from Monterey granite blocks, replacing the original adobe jail built by Walter Colton. The granite structure served as city jail for 102 years, with an enviable record of no escapes. Open to public viewing, 10-5 daily.

Underwood-Brown Adobe. Cnr. Pacific and Madison Sts. Small, 3-room single-story adobe, dating from 1843. Formerly the home of Charles Underwood, and later on that of his daughter, Margaret Brown, for whom it is named. Now part of the Few Memorial Hall and city offices complex.

Gutierrez and Miller Adobes. On Calle Principal, near Madison St. Located adjacent to each other, and sharing a common wall, the Gutierrez and Miller adobes were built in 1841 and 1872 by Mexican immigrant Joaquin Gutierrez and his son-in-law John William Miller, respectively. The Gutierrez Adobe now houses a Mexican restaurant, with a brick-paved courtyard for outdoor dining; the Miller Adobe is now privately owned, not open to the public.

Larkin House. Cnr. Jefferson St. and Calle Principal. Monterey's oldest two-story adobe, and an excellent example of the Monterey-Colonial style of architecture. Originally built in 1834 by Thomas Oliver Larkin, the first U.S. Consul to California. Now beautifully restored, with original period furnishings and decor, including many of Larkin's personal possessions. There is also a small, walled-in garden here, located adjacent to the adobe. Tours on the hour, 10-3, Wed.-Mon.; tour fee: $2.00.

Rodriguez-Osio Adobe. Located on Alvarado St., north of Franklin St. Large, two-story adobe, built in the early 1840s by Jacinto Rodriguez, businessman, one-time government offical, and delegate to California's first Constitutional Convention in 1849.

Sanchez Adobe. Alvarado St., south of Franklin St. Small, historic adobe, built in part in the 1820s by Gil Sanchez, a customs official, and enlarged, with a second story and balcony, in 1891. Largely remodeled, the adobe now houses modern shops on the ground floor.

Alvarado Adobe. At the southern end of Alvarado St. One of the oldest two-story adobes in Monterey, dating from the 1830s, charac-teristic in its Monterey style of architecture, with a second-floor balcony and a large walled-in garden. Formerly residence of Juan Bautista Alvarado, the first Monterey-born governor of California. Now a com-mercial building, housing a bank.

Cooper-Molera Adobe. Cnr. Munras and Polk Sts. One of the largest walled-in complexes in Old Monterey, encompassing 2½ acres, and comprising a two-story adobe, barn, and outbuildings. The original single-story adobe dates from 1829, built by John R. Cooper, trader, sea captain, and half brother to Thomas Larkin. The cantilevered second story, barn, and smaller outbuildings date mainly from the 1850s. The adobe now houses a Visitor Center of the Monterey State Historic Park Department, with some excellent exhibits depicting local history, as well as a small gift-cum-book shop. Tours on the hour, 10-3 daily (except Wed.); tour fee: $2.00.

Fremont Headquarters. On Hartnell St. Small, restored two-story adobe, with a balcony, and outside stairs leading to the second floor. The adobe dates from the 1840s, and pioneers Jesse and John Charles Fre-mont reportedly once occupied a wing of it. Now privately owned, and generally not open to the public.

Stevenson House. 530 Houston St. Restored, two-story adobe, dat-ing from 1840. Scottish-born writer Robert Louis Stevenson stayed here briefly in 1879, while courting his wife- to-be, Fanny Osbourne. The adobe is now part of the Monterey State Historic Park, housing period furnishings and antiques, and old manuscripts, first editions, photo-graphs, personal belongings of the author, and other Stevenson memo-rabilia. Open for public tours, 10-3 daily (except Wed.); admission fee: $2.00.

Casa Abrego. Cnr. Abrego and Webster Sts. One of Monterey's oldest landmarks, built in 1834, featuring adobe brick and wood con-struction. The single-story adobe now houses the Casa Abrego Club for Women; generally not open to the public.

Royal Presidio Chapel. Church St. Originally established as Cali-fornia's second Franciscan mission, San Carlos de Borromeo de Mon-terey, in June, 1770. The adobe chapel itself was first built in 1775, destroyed by fire in 1789, and rebuilt in 1795 with a hand-carved chalkrock figure atop the facade — that of the "Virgin of Guadalupe," the Patron Saint of Mexico. The chapel is believed to be the oldest building in existence in Monterey, in continuous use since its rebuilding in 1795. It is open to the public.

Madariaga Adobe. On Abrego St., between Webster and Church Sts. Small, single-story adobe, with connecting rooms facing the street. Built in the early American period, 1847-1848, the adobe now houses professional offices.

Estrada Adobe. Cnr. Tyler and Bonifacio Sts. A two- story adobe, originally built in the 1820's, and restored in 1961. Now preserved as an historic building.

Casa Amesti. On Polk St. Large, two-story adobe, exemplifying Monterey-Colonial architecture in California. The adobe was originally built as a one-story structure in the 1830s by Jose Amesti, a Spanish Basque, with additions made to it continuously until the 1850s. The adobe now houses a private men's club, and is open to public viewing two afternoons each week, Sat. and Sun., 2-4.

Casa De La Torre. Cnr. Jefferson and Pierce Sts. Restored, single-story adobe residence, dating from 1850. Small, sheltered garden adjoins the adobe. Now a private home; not open to the public.

Gordon House. Located on Pierce St., adjacent to Colton Hall. Early-Monterey single-story home, built entirely from wood, dating from 1849. Features an east-facing verandah, and a simple design, similar to that of the adobes of the day. Now a private residence.

Casa de Soto. Pierce St., between Jefferson and Franklin Sts. Single-story, Mexican-era adobe, dating from the 1850s. The adobe was restored in 1919, and later on, in the 1940s, occupied by novelist John Steinbeck and his family. The adobe is now part of the Monterey Institute of International Studies.

Doud House. Van Buren St., north of Scott St. New England-style wood-frame home, built in the 1860s by Francis Doud, an Irish immigrant. Now houses the exhibit rooms of the Monterey History and Art Association's costume collection.

Mayo Hayes O'Donnell Library. On Van Buren St., just north of the Doud House. Small, wooden structure, originally built in 1876 as the St. James Episcopal Church, the first Protestant church built in Monterey. In 1970, the Monterey History and Art Association acquired the historic building and restored it to house a Library of California. The library is named for a prominent member of the Association, Mayo Hayes O'Donnell. Library hours: 1.30-3.30, Wed., Fri. and Sat. Phone, (408) 372-1838.

Sherman-Halleck Adobe. Cnr. Jefferson St. and Calle Principal. Small, one-room stone and adobe structure, located in the walled-in compound of the Larkin House. The adobe dates from the 1830s, and during 1846-1847 it served as an office for the U.S. military headquarters in Monterey. Lieutenant William Sherman and Captain Henry Halleck — who later became generals in the Civil War — served under the military governor here. The adobe is now preserved as part of the Monterey State Historic Park.

House of Four Winds. On Calle Principal, near the Sherman Adobe and Larkin House. La Casa de Los Cuatro Vientos — House of Four Winds — was built in the late 1830s by Thomas Larkin, prominent Monterey businessman and first U.S. Consul to California. The adobe was named for the weathervane on its hipped roof — the first house in the area to sport a weathervane. In 1914, the Women's Civic Club purchased and restored the historic adobe. It now houses the club.

Casa Pacheco. Cnr. Abrego and Webster Sts. Mexican-era adobe, dating from the late 1820s. Casa Pacheco is now a privately-owned social club for men, generally not open to the public.

Stokes Adobe. Cnr. Hartnell, Madison and Polk Sts. Beautifully restored, two-story stone-and-adobe structure, built in the 1830s by James Stokes, an Englishman. The adobe is now a privately-owned commercial building.

French Consulate. Located on Camino El Estero, near Franklin St. Small, single-story adobe, located along the shores of El Estero. Originaly home to the French Consulate, the adobe was purchased by Jacques Antione Moerenhaut, the French Consul to California, in 1848. In 1932, the Monterey History and Art Association acquired the historic building and restored it to its original state. The adobe now houses the YWCA headquarters.

The Presidio of Monterey. Cnr. Pacific and Artillery Sts. This is the oldest of California's four Spanish presidios, located on Presidio Hill, directly above the site of Sebastian Vizcaino's landing in 1602, and the landing of Captain Gaspar de Portola and Father Junipero Serra in 1770. Features a small military museum, with displays of artifacts depicting the history of Presidio Hill during the Indian, Spanish, Mexican and American eras. Also, near the museum are the sites of Fort Mervine, a harbor fortification built in 1846 by the U.S. Army and El Castillo, a little fortress built by the Spanish government in 1792; and two monuments — one dedicated to Father Serra, and the other, a huge granite memorial, to Commodore Sloat. The Presidio is now home to the Defense Language Institute, one of the largest language schools in the world. The Presidio and Army museum are open to the public; museum hours: 9.30-4.30, Fri. and Sat.

CARMEL ART GALLERIES

Bleich of Carmel. On Dolores St. near Ocean Ave.; (408) 624-9447. Features works of American Impressionist George J. Bleich. Large selection of paintings depicting French scenes; also landscapes and seascapes of Carmel. Open daily 10.30-5.30.

Cottage Gallery at Carmel. Cnr. 6th Ave. and Mission St.; (408) 624-7888. Original paintings by renowned artists, among them Thomas Kinkade, Joyce Motazedi and K. Martell. The gallery is open 10-5 daily.

First Impressions. Dolores St. and 6th Ave.; (408) 625-5626. Specializing in contemporary printmaking, watercolors and art posters, etchings, serigraphs, lithographs and woodcuts. Hours: 10.30-5 Mon.-Sat., 11-4 Sun.; closed Tues.

GWS Galleries. 26390 Carmel Rancho Lane (opposite the Barnyard); (408) 625-2288. Exhibits of Western, wildlife, aviation, and Americana paintings by several nationally recognized artists. Gallery open 10-5.30 Mon.-Sat., 11-4 Sun.

Photography West Gallery. Ocean Ave. and Dolores St.; (408) 625-1587. Exhibits by photographers who have lived and worked on the Monterey Peninsula, including such well known names as Ansel Adams, Weston and Bullock. Also photographic books, cards and posters. Open daily 11-5.

Simic-New Renaissance Galleries, Inc. Three locations on San Carlos St. and 6th Ave.; (408) 624-7522. Wide selection of seascapes by renowned artists; also Master Impressionists' works, and wood and bronze sculpture. Open daily 10-6.

Walter White Fine Arts. San Carlos St. between 5th Ave. and 6th Ave; (408) 624-4957. Handblown art glass from Steven Carrica's California studio; also hardwood furniture, prints, paintings and paper works. Open 9.30-5.30 daily.

The Weston Gallery. 6th Ave., between Dolores and Lincoln Sts.; (408) 624-4453. Superb selection of original works by Paul Strand, Edward Weston, Ansel Adams, and other contemporary and 19th-century photographers. Hours: 10-5, Tues.-Sun.

Carmel Art Association Galleries. Dolores St., between 5th Ave. and 6th Ave; (408) 624-6176. 8-room gallery, exhibiting the finest of

Carmel's professional artists. Paintings, sculpture, graphics. Regularly changing exhibits. Gallery open 10-5 daily.

Bill W. Dodge Collection & Gallery. Dolores St. near 5th Ave.; (408) 625-5636. American primitive paintings by Bill W. Dodge and other internationally known artists. Also folk art accessories and furniture. Open daily 10-5.

Gallery Americana. Cnr. Lincoln St. and 6th Ave.; (408) 624-5071. Works of more than 50 renowned contemporary artists, including seascapes by Carmel artist Rosemary Miner. Open daily 10-5.

Zantman Art Galleries, Ltd. 6th Ave. near Mission St., and 6th Ave. near San Carlos St.; (408) 624-8314. Oldest gallery in town, established in 1959. Features paintings and sculpture by contemporary American artists, as well as selected European artists, mostly French. Open 10-5 Mon.-Sat., 11-5 Sun.

Highlands Gallery. Dolores St., between 5th Ave. and 6th Ave.; (408) 624-0535. Features wood, stone and metal sculpture by recognized West Coast sculptors. Open 11-4.30 daily.

Lindsey Gallery. Dolores St. at 5th Ave.; (408) 625-2233. Primarily paintings, featuring seascapes, landscapes, still life, harbor scenes, city scenes, rural Americana, and watercolors; some western bronze sculpture. Open 10-6 daily.

Hanson Gallery. Ocean Ave. at San Carlos; (408) 625-3111. Original oils, watercolors and limited edition serigraphs by renowned artists such as Picasso, Erte, Neiman and Pissaro. Open daily 10-5.

Casa Dolores Gallery. Carmel Plaza; (408) 624-3438. Carmel's only Western Art gallery, features original oils, watercolors and bronze sculpture. Open Mon.-Sat. 10-5, Sun. 11-4.

MONTEREY COUNTY WINERIES

Chalone Vineyard. Stonewall Canyon Rd. (P.O. Box 855), Soledad, CA 93960; (408) 678-1717. Monterey County's oldest winery, established in 1960. Produces premium, estate- grown varietal wines from its 110-acre vineyard located at the winery, at an elevation of 2,000 feet, near the Pinnacles National Monument. Wine sales and winery tours by appointment, Tues.-Fri. 10-2, Sat. 10-3.

Chateau Julien. 8940 Carmel Valley Rd., Carmel; (408) 624-2600. Housed in a picturesque replica of a rural French chateau. Offers primarily varietal, vintage-dated wines. Tasting and sales 8.30-5 Mon.-Fri., 1-4 Sat.-Sun.; tours by appointment.

Durney Vineyard. Nason Rd., Carmel Valley; (408) 659-2690/625-5433. Producer of estate-bottled varietal wines, situated on a 128-acre family-owned wine estate, high on a slope of the Santa Lucia Mountains, at the upper end of Carmel Valley. Winery visits by appointment only.

Jekel Vineyard. 40155 Walnut Ave., West Greenfield; (408) 674-5525. Well-regarded, white varietal wine producer, established in 1978. The winery is surrounded by 140 acres of estate-owned vineyards. Open 10-5 daily for tours, tasting and sales.

La Reina Winery. 29225 Gonzales River Rd., Gonzales; (408)

373-3292. A Chardonnay-only winery, founded in 1984. Open for tasting and sales by appointment; no tours.

Monterey Peninsula Winery (Tasting Room). 786 Wave St., Monterey; (408) 372-4949. Open 10-6 daily. The winery is located at 467 Shasta Ave., Sand City, (408) 394-2999, and can be visited, daily 12-5. Producer of vintage-dated varietal wines.

The Monterey Vineyard. 800 South Alta St., Gonzales; (408) 675-2316. Large, well-known Monterey County winery, housed in modern, architect-designed concrete building. Offers a full line of vintage-dated varietal wines. Art gallery on premises, featuring Ansel Adams' photographic work, entitled "The Story of a Winery"; also picnic area. Tours, tasting and sales, 10-5 daily.

Morgan Winery. 526-E Brunken Ave., Salinas; (408) 422-9855. Family owned and operated winery, producing varietal Chardonnay and Sauvignon Blanc from grapes purchased on a select-vineyard basis. Wine tasting by prior appointment; no tours or retail sales.

Roudon-Smith Vineyards (Tasting Room). 807 Cannery Row, Monterey; (408) 375-8755/(408) 438-1244 winery phone. Small, family-owned winery, located in the Santa Cruz area. Offers varietal wines primarily. Tasting room open 11-6 daily; winery tours on Saturdays, 10-4.

Smith & Hook Vineyard. 37700 Foothill Rd., Soledad; (408) 678-2132. Situated high on the eastern slopes of the Santa Lucia Mountains, with commanding views of the valley below. Estate-grown Cabernet Sauvignon is the only wine produced. Picnic area on premises; informal tours. Winery open daily 11-6.

Robert Talbott Vineyards. 1380 River Rd., Gonzales; (408) 675-3000. Small, family-owned winery, producing estate Chardonnay and Pinot Noir from its 36-acre vineyard located in the Carmel Valley. Visitors by appointment.

Ventana Vineyards (Tasting Room). 2999 Monterey-Salinas Hwy. 68, Monterey; (408) 372-7415. Tasting room housed in the Old Stonehouse of Monterey. Produces a full line of estate-bottled varietal wines, all made from grapes grown in its 300-acre vineyard located in Soledad. Tasting room open daily 12-5.

Paul Masson Vineyards (Tasting Room). 700 Cannery Row, Monterey; (408) 646-5446. One of California's oldest and largest wineries, originally established in 1852, and now a State Historical Landmark. The winery is located in the hills near Saratoga. Tasting room open 10-6 daily; wine museum on premises.

Bargetto Winery (Tasting Room). 700 Cannery Row, Monterey; (408) 475-2258. Old, family-owned winery, located in the Santa Cruz area, established in 1933. Produces varietal and fruit and berry wines. Tasting room open 11-6 daily.

RECREATION

Boating and Fishing. Boating and fishing are popular leisure activities in the Monterey Bay area, with several operators offering a variety of sportfishing trips, boat charters and whale-watching cruises. Prices

usually range from around $19.00 to $35.00 for fishing trips, depending
on the season and day of the week. For fishing trips, charters and
excursions, contact any of the following: *Randy's Fishing Trips,* 66
Fisherman's Wharf, Monterey, (408) 372-7440; *Sam's Fishing Fleet,* 84
Fisherman's Wharf, Monterey, (408) 372-0577; *Monterey Sport Fishing,* 96 Fisherman's Wharf, Monterey, (408) 372- 2203; *Chris' Fishing
Trips,* Fisherman's Wharf, Monterey, (408) 375-5951; *Suntan Charters,*
(408) 375-9895, or *Twin Otters,* Municipal Wharf, Monterey, (408)
394-4235. Also *Chardonnay Sailing Charters,* (408) 373-8664, offers
sailing day excursions and sunset cruises aboard their 70 foot yacht.

Kayaking. *Adventures By The Sea,* 299 Cannery Row, Monterey;
(408) 372-1807. Offers kayaking trips along Monterey Bay coast. *Monterey Bay Kayaks,* 693 Del Monte Ave., Monterey; (408) 373-5357.
Kayak rentals, and 2-hour as well as half-day guided tours of Elkhorn
Slough. Cost: $25.00-$50.00.

Scuba Diving. *Aquarius Dive Shop;* two locations in Monterey, at
2240 Del Monte Ave., and at 32 Cannery Row; (408) 375-1933/375-
6605. Offers full line of equipment rentals, and air; also lessons. *Bamboo Reef Enterprises,* 614 Lighthouse Ave.; (408) 372-1685; diving
lessons and equipment rentals.

Bicycling. *Adventures By The Sea,* (408) 372-1807. Custom bicycling tours for groups, with catered meals; also bike rentals. *Bay Bike
Rentals,* 640 Wave St., Monterey, (408) 646-9090. Bike rentals; 10-
speed bikes, mountain bikes and tandems; also guided tours. *Carmel
Bicycle,* 7150 Carmel Valley Rd., Carmel Valley, (408) 625-2211.
12-speed bikes available. *Freewheeling Cycles,* 188 Webster St., Monterey, (408) 373-3855. Bike rentals; 10-speed bikes and mountain bikes.

Mopeds. *Monterey Moped Adventures,* 1250 Del Monte Ave.; (408)
373-2696. Single and double seater mopeds, tour maps, practice area;
also picnic lunches available. Rates range from $10.00 an hour to $40.00
for a full day.

Ballooning. *Balloons-by-the-Sea,* 71 Myrtle Ct., Salinas; (408) 424-
0111. One-hour flights over the Salinas Valley and Monterey Bay areas;
catered gourmet picnic and champagne. Cost: $150.00 per person. Res-
ervations required.

Hang Gliding. *Western Hang Gliders,* Reservation Rd., Hwy. 1,
Marina; (408) 384-2622. Half-day flights, lessons, sales, repairs. Call
for rates for flight instruction.

Horseback Riding. *Pebble Beach Equestrian Center,* Portola Rd.,
Pebble Beach; (408) 624-2756. Escorted trail rides; 30 miles of trails.
Appointments only. *Molera Trail Rides,* Andrew Molera State Park,
Hwy. 1, Big Sur; (408) 625-8664. Trail rides along the Big Sur coast;
also sunset rides and overnight pack trips. *Monterey Bay Equestrian
Center,* 19805 Pesante Rd., Salinas; (408) 663-5712. Horse rentals, and
ocean rides; 250 acres of trails. Open daily, by appointment; $15.00 an
hour.

Tennis. Tennis facilities are available at the following locations in
the area. *Monterey Tennis Center,* 401 Pearl St., Monterey, (408)
372-0172; 6 lighted courts, lessons, pro shop. *Pacific Grove Municipal Courts,* 515 Juniper Ave., Pacific Grove, (408) 648-3130; 5
courts. *Hyatt Regency Monterey Racquet Club,* 1 Old Golf Course
Rd., Monterey, (408) 372-1234; 6 courts, open to the public; private
lessons. Call for reservations. *Mission Tennis Ranch,* 26260 Dolores
St., Carmel, (408) 624-4335; 6 courts; lessons. *Carmel Valley Rac-*

quet & Health Club, 27300 Rancho San Carlos Rd., Carmel; (408) 624-2737. 18 courts (8 lighted), lessons. *The Inn at Spanish Bay Tennis Pavilion,* 17-Mile Drive, Pebble Beach, (408) 647-7500; 8 courts; reservations required.

Tours. *A-One Chartered Limousine, Inc.,* 1425 Munras Ave.; (408) 649-1425. Group sightseeing tours of Cannery Row, 17-Mile Drive, Carmel, Big Sur and Hearst Castle. *California Heritage Tours,* 10 Custom House Plaza; (408) 373-6454. Half-day tours, daily at 1.30 p.m.; tour includes Old Monterey, Fisherman's Wharf, Cannery Row, Pacific Grove, 17-Mile Drive, Carmel Mission, and Carmel. *Otter-Mobile,* (408) 625-9782. Half-day tours of Pt. Lobos and Big Sur, the Hearst Castle, 17-Mile Drive, and the Monterey County wine country. *A Seacoast Safari,* (408) 372-1288. Tours of Monterey Peninsula, 17-Mile Drive, Hearst Castle, and the Big Sur Coast. Also, *Steinbeck Country Tours,* (408) 625-5107, offers tours of the Monterey Peninsula.

GOLF COURSES

Carmel Valley Golf & Country Club. Carmel Valley Rd., 3 miles east of Hwy. 1; (408) 624-2770. Robert Graves-designed course, located adjacent to the 5-star Quail Lodge. 18 holes, 6,175 yards, par 71. Open to Quail Lodge guests and members of other private clubs. Green fees: $105.00; $85.00 for Quail Lodge guests.

Laguna Seca Golf Club. Situated on York Road, off Hwy. 68; (408) 373-3701. Robert-Trent designed 18-hole golf course; 6,162 yards, par 72. Green fees: $45.00, $20.00 twilight special(after 2 p.m.); golf carts: $21.00. Open to the general public.

Del Monte Golf Course. Located adjacent to the Hyatt Regency Hotel in Monterey, at 1300 Sylvan Rd.; (408) 373-2436. Oldest golf course west of the Mississippi, designed by Charles Maud, and opened in 1897. 18 holes, 6,154 yards, par 72. Green fees: $40.00 regularly, $10.00 after 2 p.m.; cart rental: $20.00. Discounted rates for guests of the Hyatt and the Lodge at Pebble Beach. Carts optional.

Pacific Grove City Golf Course. 77 Asilomar Ave., Pacific Grove; (408) 648-3177. 18-hole public course; 5,500 yards, par 70. Spectacular, all-round views, with 9 greens bordering on the ocean. Green fees: $20.00/weekdays, $23.00/weekends. Carts optional. Restaurant, and driving range.

Pebble Beach Golf Links. Located adjacent to the Lodge at Pebble Beach, on the picturesque 17-Mile Drive; (408) 624-3811/624-6611. One of the most popular courses in the area, and the site of the annual AT&T National Pro-Am Golf Tournament; originally built in 1919. 18 holes, 6,806 yards, par 72. Green fees: $200.00; $150.00 for Lodge guests and Del Monte Forest residents. Rates include cart rental.

Peter Hay Par 3 Golf Course. Located at The Lodge at Pebble Beach; (408) 624-3811. 9-hole course; green fees: $7.00 all day.

Rancho Canada Golf Club. On Carmel Valley Rd., 1 mile off Hwy. 1, Carmel Valley; (408) 624-0111. Situated beside the Carmel River,

Rancho Canada offers two 18-hole championship courses, as well as a driving range. The *West Course* is 6,613 yards, par 72; the *East Course* is 6,434 yards, par 71. Green fees: $50.00, $25.00 after 2 p.m.; cart rental: $23.00.

Spyglass Hill Golf Course. Stevenson Dr. and Spyglass Hill Rd., Pebble Beach; (408) 624-6611. Famous 18-hole championship course; a favorite of golf celebrities. 6,810 yards, par 72. Green fees: $150.00; $125.00 for guests of The Lodge and NCGA members. Rates include cart rental.

The Links at Spanish Bay. Located at The Inn at Spanish Bay, at the northern end of Pebble Beach, along 17-Mile Drive; (408) 647-7500/(800) 654-9300. Newly-developed 18-hole course, modeled after the Irish and Scottish seaside courses; 6,357 yards, par 72. Green fees: $135.00, $110.00 for guests of The Inn. Rates include cart rental.

USNPS Golf Course. Located on Garden Rd., adjacent to Monterey County Fairgrounds; (408) 646-2167. 18-hole course; 5,480 yards, par 70. Open to active or retired members of the military, and guests of military personnel. Green fees: $12.00 weekdays, $15.00 weekends; Carts optional; rental $10.00.

Cypress Point Golf Course. 17-Mile Drive, Pebble Beach; (408) 624-3811/624-6611. One of the finest courses on the Monterey Peninsula, open to members only. A highlight of the course is its 16th hole, which can only be reached by driving 233 yards across open ocean. 18-hole course; 6,333 yards, par 72.

Monterey Peninsula Country Club. Pebble Beach; (408) 373-1556. Private club, formerly the site of the Bing Crosby National Pro-Am Tournament. Features two 18-hole courses; *Dunes* and *Shore*. The *Dunes Course* is 6,246 yards, par 72; the *Shore Course* is 6,334 yards, par 70. Must be played with a member. Call the club for more information.

Carmel Valley Ranch Golf Club. On Carmel Valley Rd. (approximately 7 miles inland from Carmel); (408) 625-1010. Peter Dye-designed golf course, one of the newest in the area, completed in 1981. 18 holes. Private club, for members only.

CAMPGROUNDS

Big Sur Campgrounds. Hwy. 1, Big Sur (27 miles south of Carmel); (408) 667-2322. 30 campsites, 30 RV spaces with water and electrical hookups, and 45 additional spaces for both tents and RVs. Facilities include fireplaces, restrooms, showers, a playground, laundry area, and a small store. Open year-round. Camping fee: $20.00.

Bottcher's Gap. Located in Big Sur's Palo Colorado Canyon, Palo Colorado Rd., off Hwy. 1, 10 miles south of Carmel; (805) 683-6711. 20 campsites and spaces for RVs; picnic tables, fireplaces, water, and restrooms. Also hiking possibilities. Open year-round. Camping fee: $6.00.

Cabana Holiday. 8710 Prunedale North Rd. (at Hwys. 101 and 156 West Interchange), Salinas; (408) 663-2886. 96 RV spaces with full hookups; also campsites, restrooms, showers, heated pool, store, launy, recreation room, and playground. Camping fee: $21.00.

Cypress Tree Inn. 2227 North Fremont St., Monterey; (408) 372-586. 8 RV spaces with water and electrical hookups, and laundry facilities, a hot tub and sauna, showers, restrooms, and a dump station. amping fee: $30.00.

Fernwood Resort. Hwy. 1, Big Sur; (408) 667-2422. 48 RV spaces, ith water and electrical hookups, 16 campsites, picnic tables, estrooms, showers, store, video shop, and restaurant. Also picnicking, iking, and fishing and swimming on the Big Sur River. Camping fee: 19.00-$21.00.

Fremont Peak State Park. Located near San Juan Bautista, off wy. 156; (408) 623-4255. Primitive campground with 25 campsites nd spaces for RVs, picnic tables, fire rings, water, and chemical toilets. amping fee: $8.00.

KOA Campgrounds San Juan Bautista. 900 Anzar Rd. (Hwy. 101), an Juan Bautista; (408) 623-4263. 14 spaces for RVs with full hook-ps, 27 with water and electrical hookups, and 17 campsites; other acilities include showers, flush toilets, dump station, laundromat, rec-eation room, pool, store, propane gas, picnic tables and barbeque pits. lso handicapped facilities. Camping fee: $17.50-$25.00.

Laguna Seca Recreation Area. Located near the Laguna Seca Raceway, just off Hwy. 29, at Salinas; (408) 422-6138/755-4899. 175 ampsites and RV spaces, many with water and electrical hookups; ther facilities include picnic tables, fireplaces, showers, restrooms, ump station, recreation room, and rifle range. Camping fee: $15.00-20.00.

Limekiln Beach Redwoods Campground. Hwy. 1, Big Sur; (408) 67-2403. 660-acre campground with 60 spaces for RVs and trailers, 28 ampsites, piped water, hot showers, restrooms, and a store. Also fish-ng, swimming and hiking possibilities. Campsites situated on both the each and in the redwood forest. Reservations recommended. Camping ee: $20.00.

Marina Dunes. 3330 Dunes Dr., off Reservation Rd., Marina; (408) 84-6914. 62 RV spaces with full hookups, 20 campsites, restrooms, showers, recreation room, store, and laundromat. Sand dunes and beach nearby. Camping fee: $22.00-$30.00. Reservations recommended.

Mission Farm. 400 San Juan Hollister Rd. (off Hwys. 156 and 101), San Juan Bautista; (408) 623-4456. 140 RV spaces with full hookups, including 90 pull-through spaces; also campsites, restrooms, hot show-ers, and dump stations. Camping fee: $20.00-$25.00.

Andrew Molera State Park. Hwy. 1, Big Sur, (21 miles south of Carmel); (408) 667-2315. Primitive campground in large open meadow. Facilities include picnic tables, fire rings, and chemical toilets. Short walk to beach; hiking possibilities. Camping fee: $4.00 per person.

Pfeiffer-Big Sur State Park. Hwy. 1, Big Sur; (408) 667-2315/(800) 444-7275. 218 campsites and spaces for 35-foot RVs. Facili-ties include restrooms, showers, picnic tables, laundry and store; also hiking possibilities. Open all year; reservations recommended. Camping fee: $16.00-$18.00.

Pinnacles Campground. Located 32 miles south of Hollister, near the eastern end of Pinnacles National Monument, on Hwy. 146; (408) 637-2337/389-4462. 125 campsites and RV spaces, with water and electrical hookups, hot showers, flush toilets, dump station, swimming pool and store. Camping fee: $12.00-$24.00.

Pinnacles National Monument. Located on Hwy. 146, east Soledad; (408) 389-4526. 23 primitive campsites and RV spaces (2 foot length). Facilities include picnic tables, water, fireplaces, and to lets; also some hiking possibilities. Camping fee: $6.00.

Riverside Campground. Located 27 miles from Carmel on Hwy. Big Sur; (408) 667-2414. 45 campsites and RV spaces, including 2 sites with water and electrical hookups; also restrooms, showers, fire places, playground, laundry area, dump station, nearby store, and pi nicking, swimming and fishing possibilities. Some rental cabin available. Camping fee: $19.00.

Riverside RV Park. Schulte Rd. (off Carmel Valley Rd.), (408 624-9329. 35 spaces with full hookups for RVs and trailers; als restrooms, showers, a recreation area, and nearby laundry and store Open all year; reservations advised. Camping fee: $26.00.

Saddle Mountain. Schulte Rd. (Rt. 2, Box 816), Carmel Valley (408) 624-1617. 50 campsites (25 with full hookups). Facilities includ picnic tables, barbecue pits, heated swimming pool, and hiking trails Also teepee and tent-cabin rentals. Camping fee: $17.00-$32.00.

San Lorenzo Regional Park. 1160 Broadway (off Hwy. 1), Kin City; (408) 385-5964/755-4899. 200 RV spaces — including som pull-through spaces — with full hookups; also campsites, picnic facili ties, fireplaces, restrooms, dump stations, and an historical agricultura museum and visitor center on the premises. Camping fee: $18.00 fo hookups, $12.00 for tent sites. Open all year; reservations recom mended.

San Simeon State Beach. Located 5 miles southwest of the Hears Castle, off Hwy. 1, at San Simeon; (805) 927-2068/(800) 444-7275 Offers two campgrounds: the San Simeon Creek Campground has 13 campsites and pull-through spaces for 35-foot RVs, with shower facili ties, flush toilets, piped water, fireplaces, picnic tables and a dum station; the Washburn Campground has 70 primitive campsites an spaces for 31-foot RVs, with picnic facilities, piped water and chemica toilets. Camping fee: $16.00 for San Simeon Creek; $8.00-$10.00 fo Washburn. Reservations required Apr.-Oct.

Ventana Campgrounds. Located near the Ventana Inn, off Hwy. 1 along the Big Sur coast (29 miles south of Carmel); (408) 667-2688. 62 campsites and spaces for 22-foot RVs. Picnic tables, fire rings, pipec water, showers and restrooms, and a small store nearby. Camping fee $20.00.

RESTAURANTS

(Restaurant prices — based on full course dinner, excluding drinks, tax and tips — are categorized as follows: *Deluxe*, over $30; *Expensive*, $20-$30; *Moderate*, $10-$20; *Inexpensive*, under $10.)

Monterey

Bindel's. *Expensive.* 500 Hartnell St.; (408) 373-3737. Outstanding Monterey restaurant, housed in 1840s adobe, with cozy dining rooms on two levels. Menu emphasizes California cuisine, with Pacific seafood, pasta, lamb, and duck specialties, and crepe souffles. Cocktail lounge;

ve jazz. Open for lunch and dinner daily, also Sunday brunch. Reser-
ations suggested.

Cafe Beach. *Expensive-Deluxe.* At the Monterey Beach Hotel, 2600
and Dunes Dr.; (408) 899-4544. Featuring aged beef, fresh pasta, and
esh seafood. Elegant setting; live entertainment. Open for breakfast,
unch and dinner daily.

Casa Gutierrez-Sancho Panza. *Inexpensive-Moderate.* 590 Calle
rincipal; (408) 375-0095. Traditional Mexican restaurant, housed in
ne historic Casa Gutierrez adobe. Live entertainment on weekends;
ourtyard for outdoor dining. Lunch and dinner daily.

Chef Lee's Mandarin House. *Moderate.* 2031 Fremont St.; (408)
75-9551. Mandarin cuisine. Open for lunch and dinner daily.

Clock Garden Restaurant. *Moderate-Expensive.* 565 Abrego St.;
408) 375-6100. Continental cuisine and fresh seafood; specialties in-
lude honey-glazed spareribs and shrimp fettucini. Patio for outdoor
ining; full bar. Open for lunch and dinner daily; brunch on Sundays.

Consuelo's. *Inexpensive-Moderate.* 361 Lighthouse Ave.; (408)
72-8111. Mexican restaurant, housed in two-story Victorian mansion
uilt in 1886. Offers seafood and charbroiled specialties. Patio for
utdoor dining. Open for lunch and dinner daily; brunch on Sundays.

Delfino's on the Bay. *Expensive-Deluxe.* At the Monterey Plaza
Iotel, 400 Cannery Row; (408) 646-1706. Classic regional Italian cui-
ine. Menu stresses homemade pasta and fresh seafood; many items
repared on open Genovese stove. Frequently changing entrees; exten-
ive wine list, featuring Italian and California vintages. Open for break-
ast, lunch and dinner. Reservations recommended.

Domenico's. *Expensive-Deluxe.* No. 50 Fisherman's Wharf; (408)
372-3655. Lovely setting, overlooking the yacht harbor. Features fresh
eafood entrees, mesquite-grilled meat dishes, hand-rolled pasta, and
yster bar; also homemade ice cream. Excellent wine list. Lunch and
dinner daily.

Ferrante's Restaurant & Bar. *Expensive.* At the Monterey Marriott, 350 Calle Principal; (408) 649-4234. Creative Italian cooking;
informal setting. Specialties include Focaccia bread, pasta dishes, and
fresh seafood. Spectacular bay views. Lunch and dinner daily; Sunday
buffet brunch.

The Fishery. *Moderate-Expensive.* 21 Soledad Dr.; (408) 373-6200.
Favorites here are fresh Hawaiian tuna and broiled swordfish with
saffron butter; also smoked pork ribs, and curried calamari. Open for
lunch and dinner.

Fresh Cream Restaurant. *Expensive.* 100-F Heritage Harbor, Scott
and Pacific Sts.; (408) 375-9798. Small, elegant French restaurant,
offering traditional as well as nouvelle cuisine. House specialty is Rack
of Lamb Dijon. Dinners from 6 p.m., Tues.-Sun.

Mike's Seafood Restaurant. *Moderate.* On Fisherman's Wharf;
(408) 372-6153. Italian and American cuisine, with emphasis on seafood, chicken and beef preparations. Marina views, and sunroof cocktail
lounge. Open for breakfast, lunch and dinner.

Monterey Firehouse. *Expensive.* 414 Calle Principal; (408) 649-
3016. Steak and seafood restaurant, housed in Monterey's historic First
Firehouse, built in 1897. Open for lunch and dinner daily.

Monterey Joe's Ristorante. *Moderate.* 2149 N. Fremont St., Monterey; (408) 655-3355. Italian bistro-style restaurant serving pasta, fresh
seafood, wood-baked pizzas and Italian salads. Open for lunch Mon.-

Fri., dinner daily.

Outrigger Restaurant. *Expensive.* 700 Cannery Row; (408) 37
8543. Seafood, steaks, and Polynesian specialties. Sweeping bay view
Exotic tropical drinks served in the lanai. Live entertainment on wee
ends. Open for dinner daily.

The Peninsula Restaurant. *Expensive-Deluxe.* At the Hyatt R
gency, 1 Old Golf Course Rd.; (408) 372-1234. California cuisine, wi
mesquite grill specialties and seafood and veal preparations. Restaura
overlooks the Del Monte Golf Course. Open daily for breakfast, lunc
and dinner; brunch on Sundays.

Peter B's. *Expensive-Deluxe.* At the Doubletree Hotel, 2 Porto
Plaza; (408) 649-4511. Creative California cuisine; house specialtie
include Grilled Breast of Duck with Red Wine and Currants, and Lot
ster in Wine Broth. Delicious desserts. Dinners from 5:30 p.m.

Rappa's Seafood Restaurant. *Moderate-Expensive.* On Fishe
man's Wharf; (408) 372-7562. Fresh seafood, including calama
dishes. Views of the bay and fishing harbor. Lunch and dinner daily.

Red Snapper Restaurant. *Moderate-Expensive.* Fisherman'
Wharf; (408) 375-3113. Fresh local seafood, including crab and cal
mari; also steaks, pasta and chicken. Panoramic views of the yack
harbor; cocktail lounge. Open for lunch and dinner daily. Reservation
recommended.

Sardine Factory. *Expensive-Deluxe.* 701 Wave St.; (408) 373-377£
Award-winning restaurant, featuring Old Monterey decor. Continenta
cuisine, with emphasis on fresh seafood and veal. Dinners from 4 p.m
Mon.-Sat.; also open Sundays, 2-10 p.m.

Spadaro's Ristorante. *Expensive-Deluxe.* 650 Cannery Row
(408) 372-8881. Well-known Monterey restaurant, specializing i
fine Italian cuisine. Entrees range from homemade pasta and Vea
Parmigiana to succulent, charbroiled steaks and fresh seafood an
shellfish. California wines; spectacular bay views. Open for lunch an
dinner daily.

Triples. *Expensive.* 220 Olivier St.; (408) 372-4744. California cui
sine. Located in historic home close to Fisherman's Wharf. Garden pati
for outdoor dining. Extensive wine list. Open for lunch Mon.-Sat.
dinner daily. Reservations recommended.

Whaling Station Inn Restaurant. *Moderate-Expensive.* 763 Wav
St.; (408) 373-3778. Continental cuisine, with emphasis on fresh loca
seafood, mesquite-grilled over an open-hearth, and succulent, savor
steaks. Extensive wine list. Turn-of-the-century decor. Open for dinne
5-10.30.

Wharfside Restaurant. *Moderate-Expensive.* No. 60 Fisherman'
Wharf; (408) 375-3956. Authentic Italian cuisine and fresh seafood
served in a delightful wharfside setting. Specialties include hand-rolle
ravioli and pasta, and New England clam chowder; also delicious New
York-style cheesecake and other homemade desserts. Open daily, 1
a.m.-10 p.m.

Pacific Grove

Allegro. *Inexpensive-Moderate.* Forest hill Shopping Center, Fores
Ave.; (408) 373-5770. Gourmet pizza, antipasti, pasta and salads. Oper

n.-Thurs. 11 a.m.-9 p.m., Fri.-Sat. 11 a.m.-10 p.m.

Central 1-5-9. *Expensive.* 159 Central Ave.; (408) 372-2235. California cuisine; also steaks, seafood and poultry specialties. Open for lunch Mon.-Fri., dinner daily, and brunch on Sundays.

Fandango. *Expensive.* 223 17th Street; (408) 373-0588. Informal, European-style restaurant, serving fresh seafood, pasta, paella and specialties from the mesquite grill. Open for lunch and dinner daily; Sunday lunch.

Fifi's Cafe & Bakery. *Moderate.* 1188 Forest Ave.; (408) 372-5325. Small, informal cafe with provincial French decor. Offers homemade soups, sandwiches, quiches and omelettes. Also freshly-baked pastries and desserts. Open for breakfast, lunch and dinner daily; brunch on Sundays.

First Watch. *Inexpensive.* Located in the American Tin Cannery, 125 Ocean View Blvd.; (408) 372-1125. Casual restaurant with outdoor patio, serving primarily sandwiches and omelettes. Open for breakfast and lunch daily.

Fishwife Seafood Restaurant. *Moderate.* At the Asilomar State Beach, 1996 Sunset Dr.; (408) 375-7107. Fresh seafood and pasta. Open for lunch and dinner, Wed.-Mon. Reservations recommended.

Gernot's Victoria House Restaurant. *Expensive.* 649 Lighthouse Ave.; (408) 646-1477. Continental restaurant, housed in historic Victorian mansion. Open for dinner Tues.-Sun. Reservations advised.

Melac's Restaurant. *Expensive.* 663 Lighthouse Ave.; (408) 375-7743. French country atmosphere. Specialties include salmon, sweetbreads, and lamb. Lunch Tues.-Fri., dinner Tues.-Sat., Sunday brunch. No smoking. Reservations suggested.

Michael's Grill. *Inexpensive-Moderate.* 197 Country Club Gate Center; (408) 647-8654. Casual cafe, featuring Mexican, Cajun and charbroiled specialties. Open for lunch and dinner, Mon.-Sat.

Old Bath House. *Expensive.* At Lover's Point;(408) 375-5195. Oceanside restaurant, with spectacular views. Serves primarily Continental cuisine; also seafood and steaks. Homemade desserts. Open for dinner daily. Reservations recommended.

Tavern on the Bay. *Inexpensive.* 125 Ocean View Blvd.; (408) 646-8383. Hamburgers, salads and sandwiches; some seafood dishes. Sports bar. Lunch and dinner daily.

The Tinnery. *Moderate.* Lover's Point, Ocean View Blvd.; (408) 646-1040. Casual, American-style restaurant, with outdoor patio. Open for breakfast, lunch and dinner daily. Live entertainment on weekends.

Toasties Cafe. *Inexpensive-Moderate.* 702 Lighthouse Ave.; (408) 373-7543. Casual country-style restaurant, serves primarily soups, salads, sandwiches and egg dishes. Open for breakfast, lunch and dinner daily.

Yang's Happy Family Restaurant. *Inexpensive.* 1116 Forest Ave. Pacific Grove; (408) 373-3262. Mandarin and Szechuan cuisine. Open for lunch and dinner Mon.-Sat.

Pebble Beach

The Bay Club. *Deluxe.* At The Inn at Spanish Bay, 17-Mile Drive; (408) 647-7500. Elegant dining room, featuring Northern Italian and

Mediterranean cuisine. Extensive wine list. Dinners from 6 p.m. dai
brunch on Sundays.

Club XIX. *Deluxe.* At The Lodge at Pebble Beach; (408) 624-381
Gourmet luncheons, sandwiches and salads, served in outdoor patio
a Parisian cafe setting. Dinners feature French classic cuisine, served
elegant, intimate setting. Open daily; lunch 11.30 a.m.-4.00 p.m., dinn
6.30 p.m.-10 p.m.

The Cypress Room. *Expensive-Deluxe.* At The Lodge at Pebb
Beach, 17-Mile Drive; (408) 624-3811. Contemporary California cu
sine, prepared with the freshest ingredients. Restaurant overlooks Ca
mel Bay and the 18th green at the Pebble Beach golf cours
Award-winning wine list, featuring primarily California wines. Op
for breakfast, lunch and dinner daily; brunch on Sundays.

The Dunes. *Expensive.* At The Inn at Spanish Bay, 17-Mile Driv
(408) 647-7500. Contemporary California cuisine, including a seafoc
clambake buffet on Friday nights. Spectacular ocean views. Open fc
breakfast, lunch and dinner daily.

Spanish Bay Clubhouse Bar and Grill. *Moderate.* Located next
The Links at Spanish Bay golf course on 17-Mile Drive; (408) 64
7500. Informal restaurant, serving traditional American fare. Open fc
breakfast and lunch daily.

The Tap Room. *Moderate.* At The Lodge at Pebble Beach; (408
624-3811. Casual English-style pub, serving light luncheons and dir
ners. Traditional American fare, as well as English meals. Full bar; larg
selection of beers. Open daily, 11.30 a.m.-10 p.m.

Carmel

Anton & Michel. *Expensive-Deluxe.* In the Courtyard of th
Fountains, Mission St. and 7th Ave.; (408) 624-2406. Continenta
cuisine; varied menu. House specialties include Scampi Marinara
Veal Oscar and Tournedos Rossini. California and French wines an
champagnes. Cocktail lounge; elegant setting. Open for lunch an
dinner daily.

Clam Box Restaurant. *Moderate.* Mission St., between 5th Ave
and 6th Ave.; (408) 624-8597. Popular little restaurant, family owne
and operated since 1962. Specializing in fish and chicken dishes. Casua
atmosphere. Dinners from 4.30-9 p.m., Tues.-Sun.

Creme Carmel. *Expensive.* San Carlos St. near 7th Ave.; (408
624-0444. Newer, well-regarded Carmel restaurant, specializing i
California and French cuisine, and creative homemade desserts. Ope
for dinner daily.

The French Poodle. *Expensive.* Junipero St. and 5th Ave.; (408
624-8643. Classic French cuisine; intimate setting. Restaurant estab
lished in 1961. Open for dinner; jackets required.

Guiliano's Restaurant. *Expensive-Deluxe.* Mission St. and 5th
Ave.; (408) 625-5231. One of Carmel's best- known Italian restaurants
specializing in Northern Italian cuisine. Elegant setting. Open for lunch
Tues.-Sat., dinner daily.

Hog's Breath Inn. *Moderate.* San Carlos St. and 5th Ave.; (408
625-1044. Casual, English pub-style restaurant, owned by actor-directo
Clint Eastwood. Informal American fare, featuring such entrees as th

ty Harry Burger, Mysterious Misty, Enforcer Burger and Eiger Sand-
ch! Dine in a rustic courtyard with fireplaces, or indoors. Open for
ch and dinner daily; brunch on Sundays.

Katy's Place. *Inexpensive-Moderate.* Mission, between 5th and 6th
es.; (408) 624-0199. Casual cafe, serving egg dishes, and soups,
ads and sandwiches. Open for breakfast and lunch daily.

Jack London's. *Moderate.* San Carlos St., between 5th Ave. and 6th
e.; (408) 624-2336. Casual restaurant, serving burgers, pizza, pasta
d soups. Open for lunch and dinner daily.

Pernille Restaurant. *Moderate.* San Carlos St. and 6th Ave.; (408)
4-6958. Italian restaurant, open for breakfast, lunch and dinner; also
ekend brunch.

Rio Grill. *Moderate.* 101 Crossroads Blvd.; (408) 625-5436. Nou-
le California cuisine, with oak grill specialties. Seasonally changing
nu; vintage wines by the glass. Cocktail lounge. Restaurant open for
ch and dinner daily.

Sans Souci. *Expensive.* Lincoln St., between 5th Ave. and 6th
re.; (408) 624-6220. Gourmet French restaurant, with Parisian de-
r. Favorites here are Escargot, white veal, roasted quail and Coho
lmon; also, delicious chocolate mousse. Extensive wine list, featur-
g French and California wines. Classical music. Dinners from 6
m., Thurs.- Tues.

Sassy's Bar and Grill. *Moderate.* At the Carmel Mission Inn, Hwy.
and Rio Rd.; (408) 624-3399. Continental cuisine; also buffet-style
als, and salad bar. Open for breakfast, lunch and dinner, and Sunday
unch.

The Terrace Grill. *Expensive.* At the La Playa Hotel, Camino Real
d 8th Ave.; (408) 624-4010. Elegant dining room with expansive
ews; terrace for outdoor dining. Menu stresses fresh California sea-
od. Open for breakfast, lunch and dinner daily; also Sunday brunch.

Carmel Valley

The Covey. *Expensive-Deluxe.* At Quail Lodge, 8205 Valley Greens
r.; (408) 624-1581. European cuisine, with emphasis on beef, poultry,
d fresh local seafood. Varied wine list, featuring Monterey County,
lifornia and imported wines. Rustic, country atmosphere. Dinners
om 6.30 p.m. daily; jackets required. Reservations.

From Scratch. *Inexpensive-Moderate.* Located in The Barnyard
opping center; (408) 625-2448. Features homemade food, prepared
th the freshest ingredients. Country- style dining room; patio for
tdoor dining. Open daily for breakfast, lunch and dinner; also Sunday
unch.

The Ridge Restaurant. *Expensive.* At the Robles Del Rio Lodge,
0 Punta Del Monte, Robles Del Rio; (408) 659-0170. Elegant
saurant, in spectacular setting, 1000 feet above Carmel Valley.
atures California and French cuisine; excellent wine list. Open for
nch and dinner Tues.-Sun.; also Sunday brunch. Reservations rec-
mmended.

Thunderbird Bookshop Restaurant. *Moderate.* At The Barnyard;
08) 624-9414. Informal American fare. Casual setting; books to
owse. Lunch daily, dinner Tues.-Sun.

Salinas

Gloria's Mexican Foods. *Inexpensive.* 100 Williams Rd.; (40● 424-3711. Authentic Mexican food, including fresh homemade tortill also salad bar. Open for lunch and dinner daily.

Italian Villa. *Moderate-Expensive.* 64 Monterey-Salinas Hw (408) 424-6266. Italian restaurant, featuring several specialties from ● oakwood barbeque. Lunch and dinner daily.

Mandarin Garden. *Inexpensive.* 925 N. Main St.; (408) 422-70● Szechuan and Hunan cuisine. Special family- style dinners and com nation plates. Open for lunch and dinner daily.

Michi Restaurant. *Moderate.* 42 W. Gabilan St.; (408) 424-75● Japanese restaurant, specializing in sukiyaki, teriyaki and tempura. A● sushi bar. Open for lunch and dinner, Mon.-Sat.

The Olive Garden. *Moderate.* 1580 N. Main St.; (408) 449-61● Traditional Italian cuisine, featuring fresh pasta, salads, and class Italian specialties; also homemade garlic breadsticks. Lunch and dinr daily. Reservations accepted.

Penny Farthing Tavern. *Inexpensive.* 9 East San Luis St.; (4C 424-5652. English-style pub, serving traditional British fare, includi● Fish-N-Chips, Bangers and Mash, and Cornish pasties. Wide selecti● of imported beers. Open 11 a.m.-12 p.m. daily.

Salinas Joe's. *Moderate-Expensive.* 808 N. Main St.; (408) 42● 8661. Fresh seafood, pasta, and specialties from the mesquite gr● Informal atmosphere. Open for breakfast, lunch and dinner dai● brunch on Sundays.

Big Sur

Big Sur Lodge. *Moderate-Expensive.* At the Pfeiffer-Big Sur Sta● Park, Hwy. 1, Big Sur; (408) 667-2171. Steaks, seafood and pas specialties; Monterey County wines. River views; patio for outdo dining. Breakfast, lunch and dinner daily.

Deetjen's Big Sur Inn. *Expensive.* Hwy. 1, Big Sur; (408) 66● 2377. Norwegian-style inn and restaurant, emphasizing European cu sine. Open for breakfast and dinner daily. Reservations recommende●

Glen Oaks Restaurant. *Expensive.* Hwy. 1, Big Sur; (408) 66● 2623. Well-known Big Sur restaurant, serving pasta, steaks and fre● seafood. Wooded setting. Open for dinner Tues.-Sun.; also Sund● brunch. Reservations recommended.

Lucia Lodge. *Moderate.* Hwy. 1, Lucia; (408) 667-2391/247● Ocean views. Menu features fresh seafood, steaks, soups, sandwiche● and homemade desserts. Breakfast, lunch and dinner daily.

Nepenthe. *Moderate-Expensive.* Hwy. 1, Big Sur; (408) 667-234● Spectacular cliff-top setting, with open-beamed dining room and larç outdoor terrace overlooking the ocean. Steaks and seafood. Open f● lunch and dinner daily.

Pacific Valley Center. *Inexpensive.* Hwy. 1, Pacific Valley; (80● 927-8655. Homemade soups and desserts. Open for breakfast, lunch ar dinner.

Rocky Point Restaurant. *Expensive.* Hwy. 1, Rocky Point; (408● 624-2933. Popular steakhouse, situated on clifftop, overlooking th●

The Santa Cruz Boardwalk, located at the Santa Cruz Beach, is one of the West Coast's oldest seaside amusement parks

A Big Trees Railroad steam train winds through the redwood forest near Felton, just north of Santa Cruz

Bixby Bridge, on the Big Sur coast

Sea lions basking on rocks in the Monterey Bay

Big Sur coastline. Lunch and dinner daily. Reservations recommended.

River Inn Resort. *Moderate.* Hwy. 1, Big Sur; (408) 667-2700. Rustic, riverside setting. Offers primarily American fare, with emphasis on barbeque specialties. Live entertainment on weekends. Open for breakfast, lunch and dinner daily.

Sorta Gorda. *Inexpensive.* Hwy. 1, Gorda; (805) 927-3918. Soups, burgers, and Mexican fare. Open daily 9-7 (9-5 in winter).

Ventana Restaurant. *Expensive.* At Ventana Inn, Hwy. 1, Big Sur; (408) 667-2331. One of Big Sur's most prestigious restaurants, situated on a hill above the Big Sur coast, with sweeping views of the ocean and Big Sur. Specializes in California cuisine, prepared with the freshest ingredients. Lunch and dinner daily. Reservations recommended.

San Simeon

Carriage Inn Pancake House. *Inexpensive.* 9290 Castillo Dr., San Simeon; (805) 927-8607. Open for breakfast, lunch and dinner daily.

Pezzulo's. *Moderate-Expensive.* Hwy. 1, San Simeon; (805) 927-5433. Homestyle Italian cuisine, featuring fresh pasta and seafood. Open for lunch and dinner daily. Reservations recommended.

San Simeon Restaurant. *Moderate.* 9520 Castillo Dr., San Simeon; (805) 927-4604. Ocean view restaurant, serving traditional American fare. Open for breakfast, lunch and dinner daily; cocktail lounge.

Castroville and Moss Landing

The Giant Artichoke. *Moderate-Expensive.* Hwy. 1, Castroville; (408) 633- 3204. Artichoke specialties, including french fried artichokes, artichoke cakes and artichoke hearts, marinated artichokes in salads, artichoke soup, and artichoke sausage sandwiches in pita bread. Extensive list of Monterey wines. Delicatessen and fruit stand on premises. Restaurant open for breakfast, lunch and dinner daily.

La Scuola. *Moderate-Expensive.* 10700 Merritt St., Castroville; (408) 633-2111. Italian restaurant, located in the historic Old Monterey County Schoolhouse, dating from 1860. Menu features several specialties from Tuscany, as well as artichoke preparations, polenta and rabbit. Open for lunch Tues.-Fri., dinner Tues.-Sun. Reservations recommended.

Moss Landing Oyster Bar & Co. *Moderate-Expensive.* 413 Moss Landing Rd., Moss Landing; (408) 633-5302. Fresh seafood; also homemade pasta and desserts. Open for lunch Mon.- Sat., dinner daily. Reservations recommended.

The Whole Enchilada. *Moderate.* Hwy. 1 at Moss Landing Rd., Moss Landing; (408) 633-3038. Popular area restaurant, specializing in seafood — with a Mexican flavor! Reservations recommended.

Hollister

Casa de Fruita. *Inexpensive.* Pacheco Pass Hwy., Hollister; (408) 637-2666. Restaurant features traditional American fare, such as burgers, hot turkey, spaghetti, and buffalo burgers. Also fruit and vegetable stand on premises, delicatessen and wine and gift shop. Restaurant open 24 hours.

SANTA CRUZ

"Surf City, USA"

Santa Cruz is the original "Surf City," famous for its beaches and surf and oceanfront amusement park. It has in and around it more than two dozen beaches, scores of surf shops, and even a surfing museum. It also has in it a surprisingly large collection of preserved, old Victorian homes, and a university well worth seeing, nestled amid redwoods and pasturelands, and believed to be among the loveliest campuses in California.

The Santa Cruz region, besides the city of Santa Cruz, also has other areas of interest. Directly to the north of Santa Cruz, on Highway 9, are the popular Roaring Camp and Big Trees Railroad — a 19th-century logging-era theme park — and the San Lorenzo Valley, with its redwood state parks and small, mountain towns; and just east of Santa Cruz, on Highway 1, sits the historic seaside village of Capitola, adjoined to its southeast by Aptos. Two other nearby areas of interest, northeastward from Santa Cruz on Highway 152, are Watsonville and the Hecker Pass district, the latter with a half-dozen or so small, family-run wineries, and a developed, mountain-top park.

Santa Cruz itself is located along the northern end of Monterey Bay, roughly 80 miles south of San Francisco by way of either the coastal route, Highway 1, or a combination of Highway 101 (or 280) — south to San Jose — and Route 17, southwestward.

SANTA CRUZ

Santa Cruz has a prescribed, 29-mile "Tree-Sea" tour of the city and its sights, with posted blue-and-white signs to go by, as well as three or four "Victorian Home" tours, mostly self-guided, with good maps of these available from the local Chamber of Commerce or one of the city museums. But in order to capture the true flavor of Santa Cruz, it is necessary, first of all, to go to the waterfront, where there are four beautiful, white sand beaches, some splendid ocean walks, a municipal wharf which has open-air fish markets and an array of seafood restaurants and gift shops, and — best of all — a vintage boardwalk where there is a Coney Island-type amusement park. This last, of course, is the star attraction of Santa Cruz, originally built in 1907 and believed to be the only such seaside amusement park on the West Coast. Here you will find game arcades, food concessions, souvenir shops, and twenty most thrilling rides, including a half-mile-long roller-coaster, the Giant Dipper, which is built entirely from wood, utilizing some 327,000 board feet of lumber (nearly half that required to build a small town!).

Near at hand, adjacent to the Boardwalk, is the grand old Cocoanut Grove Ballroom, the last remaining Victorian-style ballroom in Northern California, where big bands still play to thrill the young-at-heart. The ballroom was built at about the same time as the Boardwalk, in 1907, and in 1983 it underwent a $10-million renovation and conversion to a banquet and convention center. A highlight of the Cocoanut Grove is its dome-topped restaurant, the Sun Room, which features an out-sized movable glass roof that can be opened for a unique outdoor dining experience.

The mile-long sandy beach at the Boardwalk is the Santa Cruz Beach, the most popular of them all, stretching from the mouth of the San Lorenzo River — where frolicking rafters can often be seen — to the Municipal Pier farther west, beyond which lies the smaller but equally attractive Cowell Beach. Both beaches have volleyball courts, on-duty lifeguards, and swimming, surfing and sunbathing.

Two other beaches, Natural Bridges State Beach and Twin Lakes State Beach, lie to the west and east of the Santa Cruz Beach, respectively. The Natural Bridges beach, which is about a mile or so from the Boardwalk and where there are actually two or three natural, rock bridges, has a bonus. Near to it, at the west end of Delaware Avenue, is to be found the Long Marine Laboratory, part of the research facility of the Santa Cruz university, which has public tours of its aquarium and other marine exhibits, and a display of the skeleton of an 85-foot California blue whale. Also try to see the West Cliff Lighthouse at Light-

house Point on West Cliff Drive, more or less midway between
the Boardwalk and the Natural Bridges beach. It has in it a
surfing museum, filled with surfing memorabilia, including old,
wooden surfboards and vintage photographs of well-known
surfers from previous decades, and on- going video films on
surfing.

It is also an excellent idea, we might add, to drive east a little
way from the Boardwalk, on East Cliff Drive, which climbs
sharply to a point directly above the mouth of the San Lorenzo
River, where there is a grassy headland with superb views of the
Santa Cruz Beach, Boardwalk, Cocoanut Grove, the Municipal
Pier, Cowell Beach, and Lighthouse Point. Nearby, at the corner
of East Cliff Drive and Pilkington Avenue you can search out
the Santa Cruz Museum, which has displays of native birds and
fossils and Indian basketry, and a tidepool containing starfish
and sea anemones. Farther still are the Santa Cruz Harbor —
home to over 800 small craft — and the Twin Lakes State Beach
which has a lagoon that is a wildfowl refuge. These last two,
however, are not accessible on East Cliff Drive directly; it is
necessary to go north a short distance to Murray Street, and east
again, passing over the harbor, then southeastward on Lake
Avenue and the continuation of East Cliff Drive to the Twin
Lakes beach.

In any event, north of the waterfront lies downtown Santa
Cruz, which also has something in it of interest to the visitor.
The place to visit here if of course Pacific Avenue, between
Water and Lincoln streets. It is a delightful, newly-redeveloped
part of town, tree-lined and with wide sidewalks — built on the
site of the old Pacific Garden Mall which was devastated in the
1989 Loma Prieta earthquake — designed essentially for the
pedestrian. It not only has good shops, galleries, restaurants,
outdoor cafes, and hot-dog stands at intervals, but also 1960s-
style street entertainers and musicians — guitar in hand, singing
for a dime. At the Water Street end of the mall stands an old,
restored clock-tower, well worth seeing, and somewhere near
the center, just off Pacific Avenue on Cooper Street, you can
visit a most unique, eight-sided red-brick building, the Octagon
House, dating from 1882. The Octagon House is open to public
viewing and features changing art and historic exhibits.

North still is Mission Hill, a good place to view old Victorian
homes — some of the city's finest, located mainly on Mission
and High streets and Escalona Drive — and where, equally
importantly, there is a replica of the Mision la Exaltacion de la
Santa Cruz, the twelth of California's twenty-one missions
founded by Franciscan fathers. The old mission was originally
built upon the very same site, overlooking the San Lorenzo
River, in 1791.

Yet another curiosity to amaze and delight you, some three

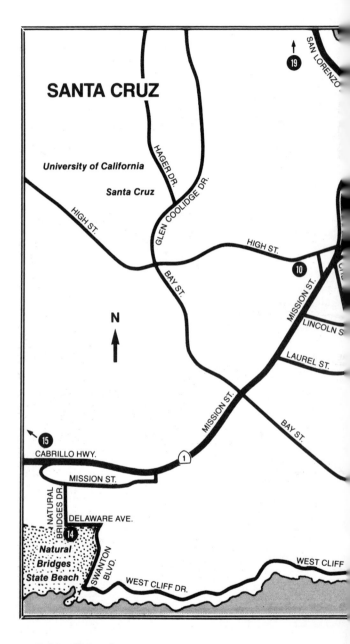

Points of Interest –
1) Santa Cruz Beach
   Boardwalk
2) Cocoanut Grove
3) Municipal Wharf
4) Yacht Harbor
5) Santa Cruz Beach

6) Cowell Beach
7) Twin Lakes State Beach
8) Santa Cruz Surfing
   Museum
9) Museum of Natural
   History

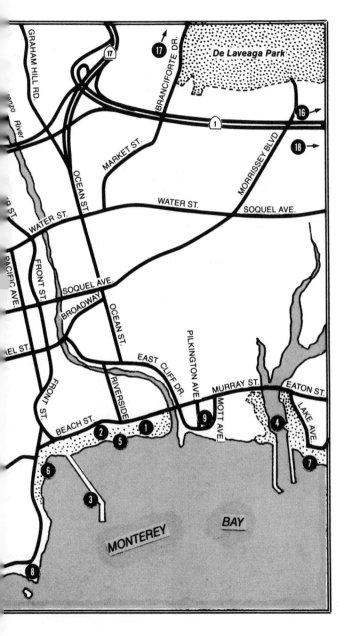

10) Mission Hill
11) Mission Santa Cruz
12) Pacific Avenue
13) Harvey West Park
14) Long Marine Laboratory
15) Wilder Ranch State Park

16) Forest of Nisene Marks
   State Park
17) The Mystery Spot
18) Capitola
19) Roaring Camp

miles or so northeast of town, off Branciforte Drive, is the frequently famous Mystery Spot. Here, in a circle roughly 150 feet in diameter, balls roll uphill, trees grow sideways, and people are unable to stand upright. It is indeed a strange natural phenomenon, that completely defies the laws of gravity. Guided tours of the circle are available daily, 10-5.

Before leaving Santa Cruz, take the time also to visit the University of California, Santa Cruz, one of the loveliest in the State, lying at the northwest edge of town, on a wooded hillside, reached primarily on High Street. The university has good programs for the performing and visual arts, as well as social and natural sciences, applied sciences, and communications courses. But the great attraction here, for students and visitors alike, has to be the campus itself, with modern, architect-designed buildings tucked away among groves of noble redwoods, and surrounded, quite randomly, by the equally lovely, rolling pasturelands. Detailed maps of the campus can be obtained at the university, together with directions for touring the wooded grounds.

SAN LORENZO VALLEY

North of Santa Cruz lies the scenic San Lorenzo Valley, reached primarily on Highway 9, a mountainous sort of road that journeys alongside the San Lorenzo River for the most part, passing by groves of towering pines and redwoods. The valley's chief towns, of course, are Felton, Ben Lomond and Boulder Creek — all of them small, secluded, and in picturesque forest settings.

Felton, which lies roughly 10 miles north of Santa Cruz, is the southernmost of the towns in the valley. But before Felton, there are two places of supreme tourist interest—the 4,300-acre Henry Cowell Redwood State Park, just a mile or so to the south of Felton, which offers in it some delightful nature walks through groves of virgin, 200-year-old redwoods; and Roaring Camp, an 1880s logging camp, named for its one-time boisterous community, and which also has in it the Big Trees Railroad, a 19th-century steam train that offers excursions through miles of magnificent redwood forests. Roaring Camp also features a recreated Western-style village, with a country store, steam sawmill and railroad depot, and hosts several special events, including chuck-wagon barbeques, moonlight picnics, bluegrass music, and melodrama theater.

At Felton itself there is a covered bridge, one of the few remaining in California, dating from 1892 and now a State Historical Landmark. The bridge is 140 feet long and 34 feet

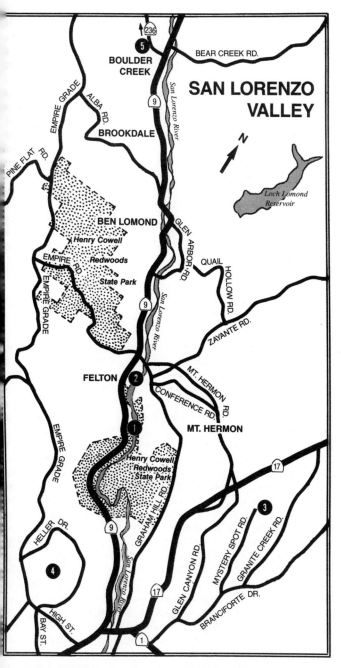

Points of Interest-
1) Roaring Camp and Big Trees Railroad
2) Felton Covered Bridge
3) Mystery Spot
4) University of California, Santa Cruz
5) Big Basin Redwoods State Park

high, believed to be the tallest such bridge in the country. The bridge is open to foot traffic; there is also a picnic area adjacent to the bridge.

Above Felton, two miles, is Ben Lomond, a village, no more, but with something in it that is reminiscent of Scotland. Ben Lomond, in fact, has its very own stone castle, the Waverly Castle, located near the north end of town, just off the highway. The castle, however, is privately owned, and not open to the public.

North still, another two or three miles, and we are at Boulder Creek, a typical mountain town, with a handful of shops strung along its main street (Highway 9), where local artisans display and sell their handicrafts. There is also a small public park here, the Boulder Creek Park, with a playground and picnic area.

Of interest, too, six miles north from Boulder Creek on Highway 236, is the Big Basin Redwood State Park, a 16,000-acre forest preserve, which also has the distinction of being California's first state park, originally founded in 1902. The park has over 80 miles of hiking trails, journeying through lush, wooded country, and a small nature museum, with exhibits of plants and animals of the region. There is also a primitive campground here, and ranger-organized campfire programs during the summer months, featuring slide shows and movies, and lectures of interest to nature buffs.

CAPITOLA AND NEARBY

Some two or three miles east of Santa Cruz on Highway 1 lies Soquel, a small town situated to the north of the highway, but with very little in it of visitor interest; and just to the south of there — south of the highway — is Capitola, a picturesque little beach community, claimed to be the oldest seaside village in California, dating from 1880. Capitola's chief attraction, of course, is its beach, where there is also a freshwater lagoon and an ancient, 150-year-old wharf which is now a designated fishing pier. There is also a marina here, and fishing boat rentals, and in September each year the wharf area is the site of some of the events of Capitola's colorful Begonia Festival, with the "Begonia Boat Races" finishing in the lagoon here. Also, directly above the Capitola Beach is the Esplanade, circling the waterfront for the most part, and dotted with several well-liked bars and restaurants, including the monstrously popular Margaritaville. Capitola, besides, has a fine collection of restored Victorians and smaller, brightly-colored oceanfront cottages, all of which go to add to the flavor of the oceanside village.

Two other beach areas of interest here, lying just to the east

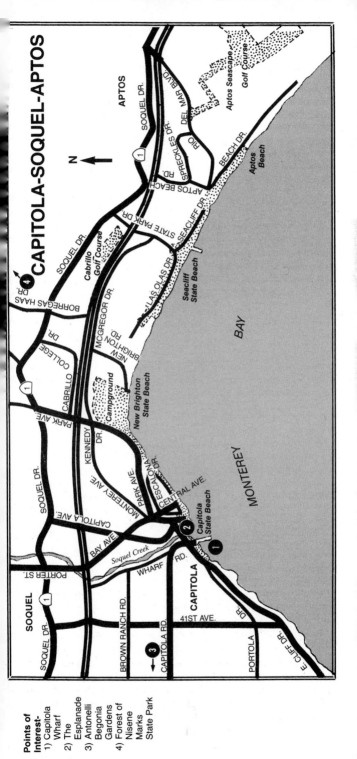

CAPITOLA-SOQUEL-APTOS

N

Points of Interest-
1) Capitola Wharf
2) The Esplanade
3) Antonelli Begonia Gardens
4) Forest of Nisene Marks State Park

107

of Capitola, a mile or two distant, are New Brighton and Seacliff
Both have good sandy beaches, and picnicking and camping
facilities. Seacliff, in addition, has a unique pier, comprising a
435-foot-long cement ship, the *Palo Alto*.

East still, lies Aptos, also with a sandy beach — which, in
fact, adjoins the Seacliff State Beach — and two golf courses
Of particular interest here, however, just to the north of Aptos,
a little over two miles, is the Forest of Nisene Marks State Park,
a splendid, 10,000-acre redwood park, where you can view the
remnants of an ancient Chinese labor camp, and where, also, the
epicenter of the Loma Prieta earthquake — which, on October
17, 1989, devasted parts of Santa Cruz and caused significant
damage in the San Francisco Bay Area — is located. There are
several miles of scenic hiking trails in the park, including a
1½-mile trail that leads to the epicenter area. The park can be
reached by way of Soquel Drive — which parallels Highway 1,
to the north — then Aptos Creek Road northward, directly into
the park.

DETOURS

Watsonville

Watsonville, lying in the heart of the fertile Pajaro Valley,
some 12 miles southeast of Santa Cruz on Highways 1 and 152,
also has something in it of interest. It is, of course, an important
agricultural center, notable for its fall apples and berries in
summer — strawberries, raspberries and ollalieberries — with
a fair number of the local farms offering fruit picking in season.
It is also, equally importantly, an historic town, dating from the
mid-1800s, with several old and lovely buildings, many of them
located in the downtown area. Notable among these are the
Mansion House and the Lettunich Building, both located on
Main Street and dating from the early 1900s; the lovely St.
Patrick's Church, also on Main Street, characteristic in its
Gothic architecture and the unique Tuttle Mansion. Also of
interest is the William H. Volck Museum on East Beach Street,
housed in the turn-of-the-century home of William H. Volck,
developer of modern pesticides and acknowledged as the "savior of the apple industry" in the Pajaro Valley. The museum has
permanent and changing displays of local historical interest,
including a superb collection of 19th-century costumes and old
photographs, antique dolls, ladies' glove boxes, and other such
items. There is also a small library and archive on the premises,
housing, besides books on local history, some rare, historical
documents. The museum is operated and maintained by the

Pajaro Valley Historical Association, which, by the way, also publishes a brochure detailing a self-guided walking tour of Watsonville's historic district, available at the museum, or from the local Chamber of Commerce on Freedom Boulevard.

Watsonville also has in it the Santa Cruz County Fairgrounds, located just off the highway (152), northeast of town, and where several worthwhile events are scheduled year-round, including the Santa Cruz County Fair in September, the Strawberry Festival in June, and the Watsonville Antique Fly-In in May, which features displays of vintage airplanes and colorful aerobatics.

Hecker Pass

Another detour, northeastward from Watsonville, is the Hecker Pass area, reached on the Hecker Pass Road (Highway 152), a mountainous sort of road which journeys over the 1300-foot Hecker Pass, northeastward to Gilroy, passing by the 4000-acre Mount Madonna Park, which has some picnicking and hiking possibilities. The Hecker Pass region itself is quite lovely, nestled in the hills above Watsonville, and with a dozen or so small, mostly family-owned-and-operated wineries, among them the Hecker Pass and Thomas Kruse wineries, Sarah's Vineyard, Fortino, Live Oaks, Conrotto, and Kirigin Cellars. Most of the wineries are open to the public for wine tasting and retail sales, with some of them also offering winery tours and picnic areas overlooking hillside vineyards.

Gilroy

Also worth visiting in the area, some 18 miles or so northeast from Watsonville on Highway 152 — the Hecker Pass route — at the intersection of Highway 101, is Gilroy, the celebrated "Garlic Capital of the World." Gilroy produces nearly 90% of the nation's garlic, and in July each year, usually during the third week of the month, the town hosts a week-long Garlic Festival, cooking more than 4,000 pounds of the "stinking rose" in a variety of foods, and offering all types of garlic products for sale — everything from garlic braids and garlic breads, to garlic wines, garlic perfumes and even garlic ice-cream. For first-time visitors to the area, a place of special interest is the "Garlic World," located on Highway 101, just to the south of Gilroy; it has garlic in every form, flavor and quantity, as well as books on garlic and garlic cooking, and all sorts of other garlic products. Nearby, too, is the Rapazzini Winery, located just south of Garlic World, also on the highway, and which makes, besides varietal grape wines, a notable Garlic Dinner Wine and other exotic garlic specialties.

PRACTICAL INFORMATION FOR SANTA CRUZ

HOW TO GET THERE

Santa Cruz

There are several different routes leading from San Francisco to Santa Cruz, which lies approximately 80 miles to the south, along the northern edge of picturesque Monterey Bay. The most commonly used is, of course, *Highway 101* — or *Highway 280* — southeast to Santa Clara (47 miles), then directly south on *Highway 17*, 13 miles, to Santa Cruz.

A more scenic, though somewhat longer, route is by way of *Highway 1*, south along the coast, to Santa Cruz. It is approximately 84 miles by way of the coastal route.

San Lorenzo Valley

The San Lorenzo Valley lies just to the north of Santa Cruz, reached directly on *Highway 9*. Felton, the southernmost of the valley towns, is roughly 10 miles from Santa Cruz; Ben Lomond is 2 miles to the north of there; and Boulder Creek, another 2½ miles north of Ben Lomond.

Capitola, Soquel and Aptos

Capitola, Soquel and Aptos lie immediately to the east and southeast of Santa Cruz, with Capitola and Aptos strung along *Highway 1*, along Monterey Bay, and Soquel located directly to the north of Capitola, also on *Highway 1*. Capitola and Soquel are 2 miles from Santa Cruz, and Aptos, 6 miles.

TOURIST INFORMATION

Santa Cruz County Conference and Visitors Council, 701 Front St., Santa Cruz; (408) 425-1234/(800) 833-3494. Variety of tourist brochures and free publications; also maps for walking tours of Victorian homes, and museum guide. Accommodation and restaurant guides, calendar of events. Open daily 9-5. Also, *Bed & Breakfast Innkeepers* *f Santa Cruz County*, (408) 425-8212, offers a referral service for local nns.

Scotts Valley Chamber of Commerce, 10 Camp Evers Lane, Scotts Valley, 95067; (408) 438-1010. Maps, and visitor-interest brochures for area attractions, accommodations and restaurants.

Capitola Chamber of Commerce, 621B Capitola Ave., Capitola; 408) 475-6522. Maps and tourist literature, including information on he famous Begonia Festival and other annual events.

Aptos Chamber of Commerce, 9099 Soquel Dr., No. 12, Aptos; 408) 688-1467. Locally-published brochure, with area map and information on the area's history, seasonal events, and accommodations and restaurants.

Watsonville Chamber of Commerce, 801 Freedom Blvd., Watsonville; (408) 724-3900. Variety of visitor information, including brochures on tours of area wineries and farms, and self-guided walking tour maps of Watsonville's historic district.

Gilroy Chamber of Commerce/Visitors Bureau, 7780 Monterey St., Gilroy; (408) 842-6436. Calendar of events and other tourist literature, including information on area lodgings, restaurants, wineries and other places of interest, and local specialty shops.

ACCOMMODATIONS

Santa Cruz

Aladdin's Inn. *$35-$45.* 50 Front St.; (408) 426-3575. 23 units, with TV and phones; some kitchenettes, and ocean views. Close to Municipal Wharf and Boardwalk.

All Suites Inn Best Western. *$75-$95.* 500 Ocean St.; (408) 426-8333/(800) 528-1234. 40 units, with TV, phones, refrigerators and microwave ovens; some ocean-view rooms, with fireplaces. Also pool, and jacuzzi. Continental breakfast.

Harbor Inn. *$45-$55.* 645 7th Ave.; (408) 479-9731. 17 units, including some in a remodeled farmhouse. TV, phones, kitchenettes.

Best Western Inn. *$49-$85.* 126 Plymouth St.; (408) 425-4717/(800) 528-1234. 26 units; TV, phones, refrigerators, hot tub and sauna.

Best Western Torch-Lite Inn. *$45-$65.* 500 Riverside Ave.; (408) 426-7575/(800) 528-1234. 38 units; TV, phones, pool. Close to beach.

Blackburn House. *$30-$60.* 101 Cedar St.; (408) 423-1804. 31 units, including some cottages and cabins. TV, phones, kitchenettes.

Blue-Bird Motel. *$45-$70.* 2-1345 East Cliff Dr; (408) 475-3381. 9 units, with TV and phones; some kitchenettes. Close to beach.

Candlelite Inn. *$30-$80.* 1101 Ocean St.; (408) 427-1616. 42 units, with TV and phones; non-smoking rooms available. Restaurant; pool.

Carousel Motel. *$55-$95.* 110 Riverside Ave.; (408) 425-7090. Located directly across from the beach and Boardwalk. 34 rooms with balconies; TV and phones.

Casa Blanca Motel. *$95-$185.* 101 Main St.; (408) 423-1570. 27

units, some with fireplaces and private balconies with ocean views. TV phones; gourmet restaurant on premises.

Chaminade. *$150-$175.* 1 Chaminade Lane; (408) 475-5600. 15? rooms; TV, phones, pool, spas, fitness center, 4 tennis courts, and ? nature trail. Also 2 restaurants on premises.

Comfort Inn. *$79-$99.* 110 Plymouth St.; (408) 426-2664. 52 units TV, phones, wet bars and refrigerators; some fireplaces. Pool, spa and sauna. Complimentary breakfast.

Dream Inn By-The-Sea. *$105-$195.* 175 W. Cliff Dr.; (408) 426-4330/(800) 662-3838. 163-room beachfront hotel; TV, phones, private balconies with bay views. Jacuzzi, pool, and 2 restaurants. Non-smoking rooms available.

Edgewater Beach Motel. *$65-$175.* 525 Second St.; (408) 423-0440. 20 units, some with ocean views; also some fireplaces. TV, phones, pool.

Hitching Post Motel. *$45-$65.* 1717 Soquel Ave.; (408) 423-4608. 31 units, including some studio units with kitchens. TV; pool.

Holiday Inn. *$69-$97.* 611 Ocean St.; (408) 426-7100/(800) 241-1555 in California. 170 rooms; TV, phones, pool, jacuzzi, coffee shop, restaurant and cocktail lounge with weekend entertainment. Non-smoking rooms available. Handicapped facilities.

The Inn at Pasatiempo. *$89-$175.* 555 Hwy. 17; (408) 423-5000. 56 units, including 4 suites; TV, phones, pool and restaurant. Complimentary breakfast. Located adjacent to golf course.

Lanai Motor Lodge. *$50-$125.* 550 Second St.; (408) 426-3626. 20 units, some with kitchenettes. TV, phones, sundecks, and pool. Ocean views.

La Plaza Motel. *$35-$40.* 506 Riverside Ave.; (408) 426-2899. 24 units; some suites with kitchenettes. TV, phones, pool and jacuzzi.

Magic Carpet Motel. *$45-$120.* 130 W. Cliff Dr.; (408) 423-7737. Located across from the beach and Boardwalk. 28 rooms, some with ocean views; jacuzzi.

Mission Inn. *$85-$100.* 2250 Mission St.; (408) 425-5455. 42 units, including 4 suites; phones, TV, hot tub, sauna. Some non-smoking rooms.

Monterey Manor. *$60-$75.* 325 Pacific Ave.; (408) 423-8564. 37 units with TV; some kitchenettes. Pool and sundeck. Continental breakfast.

Ocean Echo Motel & Cottages. *$65-$95.* 401 Johans Beach Dr.; (408) 462-4192. 4 units, 5 studios, 6 cottages. Kitchenette units available; also some units with balconies and views. TV, phones; private beach.

Pacific Inn. *$39-125.* 330 Ocean St.; (408) 425-3722. 36 units with TV, phones, and refrigerators; some units with whirlpool baths. Indoor pool. Handicapped facilities.

Riverside Garden Inn. *$48-$90.* 600 Riverside Ave.; (408) 458-9660/(800) 527-3833. 80 units with TV and phones; some balconies. Also pool, and spas. Continental breakfast.

Salt Air Motel. *$40-$70.* 510 Leibrandt Ave.; (408) 423-6020. 26 units, with TV, phones, and kitchenettes. Pool. Close to beach and Boardwalk.

Sandpiper Lodge. *$40-$79.* 111 Ocean St.; (408) 429-8244. Located close to the beach and Boardwalk. 25 rooms, with TV, phones, and hot tubs. Continental breakfast.

Santa Cruz Inn. *$50-$85.* 2950 Soquel Ave. (at Hwy. 1); (408) 475-6322. 20 units with TV and phones; some units with jacuzzis and fireplaces.

Santa Cruz Travelodge. *$58-$85.* 525 Ocean St.; (408) 426-2300/(800) 255-3050. 55 units; phones, TV, pool, non-smoking rooms. Handicapped facilities.

St. Charles Court. *$50-$75.* 902 3rd St., (408) 423-2091. 28 rooms and suites; TV, phones. Heated pool.

Seaside Lodge. *$38-$68.* 301 Beach St.; (408) 426-0420. Located across from the beach and Boardwalk. 30 units, with TV. Some ocean views. Pool.

Travelodge Riviera. *$45-$85.* 619 Riverside Ave.; (408) 423-9515. 62 units, including 20 suites, and some kitchenette units. Phones and TV; hot tub, spa, pool, non-smoking rooms.

Victorian Inn Motel. *$50-$70.* 516 Water St.; (408) 426-6111. 50 units; TV, phones, pool. Close to beach. Restaurant across the street.

West Wind Motel. *$45-$110.* 204 Second St; (408) 426-7878. 50 units, including some suites and some kitchenette units. TV, phones, sundeck and pool. Located directly across from the Boardwalk.

San Lorenzo Valley

Ben Lomond Hylton. *$52-$70.* Hwy. 9, Ben Lomond; (408) 336-2292. 21 units with TV and phones. Pool. Restaurant nearby.

Best Western Inn Scotts Valley. *$60-$80.* 6020 Scotts Valley Dr., Scotts Valley; (408) 438-6666/(800) 528-1234. 58 units with TV, phones, and refrigerators. Pool, spa. Restaurant adjacent.

Brookdale Lodge. *$50-$130.* 11570 Hwy. 9, Brookdale; (408) 338-6433. Historic, 46-room lodge, built in the late 1800s, nestled among redwoods. Some suites available; TV. Restaurant on premises.

Fern River Resort Motel. *$50-$75.* 5250 Hwy. 9., Felton; (408) 335-4412. 13 cabins in wooded setting, situated along the San Lorenzo River, adjacent to Henry Cowell State Park. Kitchenettes, some fireplaces, picnic and barbecue facilities.

Jaye's Timberlane Resort. *$65-$95.* 8705 Hwy. 9, Ben Lomond; (408) 336-5479. 10 one- and two-bedroom cottages with TV and kitchens; some fireplaces. Pool.

Merrybrook Lodge. *$68-$88.* 13420 Big Basin Way, Boulder Creek; (408) 338-6813. 6 cabins with kitchens; some fireplaces. Located among redwoods, near creek.

Tyrolean Inn. $41-$56. 9600 Hwy. 9, Ben Lomond; (408) 336-5188. 7 cabins in wooded setting; TV, and kitchenettes. ˙

Capitola and Aptos

Best Western Seacliff Inn. *$89-$115.* 7500 Old Dominion Court, Aptos; (408) 688-7300/(800) 367-2003. 140 units; TV and phones, restaurant, cocktail lounge, spa, pool, putting green, and koi pond. Non-smoking rooms available.

Capitola Inn. *$85-$125.* 822 Bay Ave., Capitola; (408) 462-3004. 56 rooms, with TV, phones, decks and patios; some kitchenette units.

Heated pool.

Capitola Venetian Hotel. *$70-$150.* 1500 Wharf Rd., Capitola; (408) 476-6471/(800) 332-2780. 22 units, with TV, phones, and kitchenettes; some ocean views, and balconies and fireplaces. Close to beach.

Harbor Lights Motel. *$75-$125.* 5000 Cliff Dr., Capitola; (408) 476-0505. 10 units, with TV, phones, and private balconies with views of Capitola Beach and Monterey Bay. Centrally located.

Rio Sands Motel. *$50-$80.* 116 Aptos Beach Dr., Aptos; (408) 688-3207/(800) 826-2077. 50 units with TV and phones; some kitchenettes. Pool, garden spa, picnic and barbecue area. Complimentary breakfast. Close to beach.

Watsonville

Best Western Inn. *$44-$94.* 740 Freedom Blvd.; (408) 724-3367/(800) 528-1234. 42 units, with TV, phones, and refrigerators. Pool, jacuzzi. Handicapped facilities.

El Rancho Motel. *$35.* 976 Salinas Rd.; (408) 722-2766. 12 units, with TV and phones; some kitchenettes.

Star Motel. *$35-$65.* 584 Arthur Rd.; (408) 724-4755. 30 units; TV, phones.

Pajaro Dunes. *$160-$450.* 2661 Beach Rd.; (408) 722-4671. Resort development with vacation rental homes and condominiums. Phones, TV, fireplaces, kitchens. Tennis courts, volleyball, basketball, hiking and jogging trails, beach. Close to Pajaro Valley Golf Course. 2-night minimum stay.

BED & BREAKFAST INNS

Santa Cruz

Cliff Crest. *$80-$125.* 407 Cliff St.; (408) 427-2609. 1890s home in garden setting, built by former Lieutenant Governor of California, William Jeter. 5 antique-filled rooms with private baths; complimentary wine and cheese. Central location.

Babbling Brook Inn. *$85-$135.* 1025 Laurel St.; (408) 427-2437. 12 guest apartments, with balconies and fireplaces; also private baths, TV and phones. Parlor and registration areas date from the early 1900s. Full breakfast.

The Darling House. *$85-$115.* 314 West Cliff Dr.; (408) 458-1958. Spanish Revival-style home near Lighthouse Point, with views of wharf and Boardwalk areas. 6 rooms, most with fireplaces; also one cottage behind the main house, with accommodations for four. The house dates from 1910.

Chateau Victorian. *$99-$131.* 118 First St.; (408) 458-9458. 7 comfortable rooms in one of Santa Cruz's turn-of-the-century homes. Lovely ocean views; close to beach, wharf and Boardwalk. Continental breakfast, with fresh fruit, croissants and muffins; wine and cheese in the evening. No smoking.

New Davenport Bed & Breakfast. *$65-$105*. 31 Davenport Ave., Davenport; (408) 425-1818. 12 rooms, decorated with antiques. Gift shop and casual restaurant on premises. Continental breakfast. No smoking.

Pleasure Point Inn. *$95-$125*. 2-3665 East Cliff Dr.; (408) 475-4657. 4 guest rooms, decorated in a beach motif with antiques and wicker; private baths; some ocean views. Continental breakfast.

San Lorenzo Valley

Chateau Des Fleurs. *$90-$100*. 7995 Hwy. 9, Ben Lomond; (408) 336-8943. 1870s estate, formerly owned by the Bartlett family, of Bartlett pears fame. 3 rooms in the main house, with a guest cottage at the rear. Full breakfast, and hors d'oeuvres in the evening. No smoking.

Fairview Manor. *$79-$99*. 245 Fairview Ave., Ben Lomond; (408) 336-3355. Country inn, set on 3 wooded acres beside the river. 5 rooms, with private baths. Full breakfast.

Capitola, Soquel and Aptos

Bayview Hotel. *$80-$90*. 8041 Soquel Dr., Aptos; (408) 688-8654. 7 guest rooms, furnished with original Victorian antiques; private baths. Complimentary breakfast. Restaurant on premises. No smoking.

Apple Lane Inn. *$76-$136*. 6265 Soquel Dr., Aptos; (408) 475-6868. Restored Victorian farmhouse, set among vineyards and orchards. 5 rooms, some with private baths. No smoking.

Mangels House. *$89-$115*. 570 Aptos Creek Rd., Aptos; (408) 688-7982. Beautifully restored 1880s Southern Mansion, former home of industrialist Claus Mangels. Wooded setting. 5 rooms. Full breakfast.

Inn at Depot Hill. *$155-$250*. 250 Monterey Ave., Capitola; (408) 462-3376. 8-room inn, with European theme decor, housed in former, turn-of-the-century railroad depot. Private baths, fireplaces, TV and phones. Full breakfast; hors d'oeuvres, cookies, and port in the evenings.

Blue Spruce Inn. *$80-$125*. 2815 South Main St., Soquel; (408) 464-1137. 3 antique-decorated rooms in main house and carriage house; private baths, hot tub. Full breakfast.

Watsonville

Dunmovin Bed & Breakfast. *$65-$75*. 1006 Hecker Pass Rd., between Watsonville and Gilroy; (408) 722-2810. Situated on a hill overlooking Watsonville Valley. 3 rooms with private baths; hot tub, tennis court. Full breakfast, complimentary wine.

SEASONAL EVENTS

January

Second Weekend. *Fungus Fair.* Held at the Santa Cruz City Museum. Wild mushroom tastings, displays, and variety of foods made with mushrooms. (408) 429-3773.

February

Fourth Weekend. *Clam Chowder Cook-Off.* Held at the Santa Cruz Beach Boardwalk. Decorated booths and food stalls, featuring Manhattan- and Boston- style clam chowder. More information on (408) 423-5590/429-3477. *Santa Cruz Baroque Festival.* Held at the First Congregational Church, Santa Cruz. Festival runs through February and March, and features recitals of baroque music. For a complete schedule, call (408) 476-2313.

March

Third Weekend. *Great Train Robberies.* At Roaring Camp, Felton. Re-enactment of Old West days, with lawmen and desperados, train robberies, dueling, shootouts; also stagecoach rides. Events are scheduled for 3rd and 4th weeks of the month. For a program, call (408) 335-4484.

April

Second Weekend. *Amazing Egg Hunt.* Easter celebration, in Felton. Nearly 10,000 colorful Easter eggs are hidden in the Roaring Camp redwood forest atop Bear Mountain; prizes awarded for finding specially marked eggs. (408) 355-4484. *Spring Wildflower Show.* At the Santa Cruz City Museum, Thursday through Sunday. Display of several hundred wildflowers native to California. (408) 429-3773.

May

First Weekend. *Cinco de Mayo Celebration.* At the Santa Cruz County Fairgrounds in Watsonville. Features roaming mariachi bands, Mexican dances, booths and food concessions, and a textile art show. Call (408) 722-7067 or 725-2394 for more information.
Fourth Weekend. Annual Longboard Club Invitational. At Cowell Beach. Surfing competitions, featuring some of the country's best-known surfers. (408) 429-3477. *Harbor Festival & Boat Show.* At the Santa Cruz Yacht Harbor. Boat show and boat parade; dinghy, bathtub,

kayak, and sailboat races; also live music, food concessions, booths selling boating equipment, and arts and crafts show. Free admission. *West Coast Antique Fly-In and Air Show.* Watsonville Airport. Second largest antique fly-in and air show in the nation. View antique planes and military aircraft and experimental aircraft. Daily airshows and aerobatic displays. Admission: $6.00 adults, $3.00 children. For more information, call (408) 724-3849. *Civil War Re-Enactment.* Held at Roaring Camp, Felton. Features hundreds of uniformed soldiers in re-enactment of Union-Confederate battles and mid-1800s camp life; largest such encampment on the West Coast. Also, 1860s fashion show. (408) 335-4484.

June

First Weekend. *Redwood Mountain Faire.* Arts and crafts show, held at the Highlands Park in Ben Lomond. Displays of arts and crafts, theatrical performances, and food stalls. (408) 336-2055.

Second Weekend. *Jose Cuervo Volleyball Tournament.* Santa Cruz Beach, Santa Cruz. 32 of the world's best 2-man beach volleyball teams compete for $20,000 in prize money. Also women's swimsuit contest. (213) 450-4417

Third Weekend. *Cherry Jubilee.* At Casa de Fruita, Hollister. Celebration of region's cherry harvest; features gourmet foods, entertainment, exhibits, contests and wine tasting. Call (408) 637-0051 for information on events. *Burrito Bash.* At the Santa Cruz County Fairgrounds, Watsonville. Competition for the best and the biggest burrito, and burrito-eating contest; entertainment and 10-kilometer run from Pinto Lake. Admission fee: $1.00. For more information, call (408) 724-5671. *Fats Waller Memorial Jazz Festival.* Held in Watsonville. Professional jazz bands perform at a half-dozen different sites throughout town, featuring jazz from the late 1800s and early 1900s; also food concessions. (408) 728-3948.

Fourth Weekend. *Strawberry Festival.* Santa Cruz County Fairgrounds, Watsonville. Two-day festival, celebrating the area's strawberry harvest. Live entertainment, arts and crafts show, 10-kilometer run, and strawberries prepared in every imaginable way. (408) 688-3384.

July

First Weekend. *Fourth of July Celebration.* Harvey West Park, Santa Cruz. Festivities include a chili cook-off and Firecracker 10-kilometer race. (408) 429-4377. Aptos 4th of July Parade. In downtown Aptos. Shortest Fourth of July parade in the nation — 100 yards. Residents and visitors alike participate, dressed in colorful costumes. Phone, (408) 688-2428.

Second Weekend. *Handcar Races and Steam Festival.* Roaring Camp, Felton. Some of California's best railroad handcar racing teams compete on 300 meters of Santa Cruz Big Trees Railroad track. Winners advance to U.S. Nationals, held in Sacramento. The festival also has displays of rare, old steam and gas-powered railroad and industrial equipment. (408) 335-4484.

Third Weekend. *Beach Street Revival.* At Beach Street and th
Boardwalk in Santa Cruz. 50's and 60's nostalgic festival, with
50's-style rock 'n roll dance at Cocoanut Grove. Other events include
Miss Beach Street contest, the Soho Soda Grand Cruise Car Parade, an
a car show and auction. For schedule of events, call (408) 438-1957.

Fourth Weekend. *Wharf to Wharf Run.* 10,000 runners participat
in a 6-mile run along the coast, from the Santa Cruz Wharf to th
Capitola Wharf. Beach party at the finish, with refreshments. Entry fee
$10.00. For more information, call (408) 427-0242/475-2196. *Gilro*
Garlic Festival. Gilroy. 3-day celebration of Gilroy's garlic heritage
variety of garlic foods and garlic products, continuous entertainment
garlic gallop, and coronation of Miss Garlic Festival. (408) 842
1625/842-6437. *Estival Festival.* Held in July and August at variou
locations in Santa Cruz. 20 of Santa Cruz County's top groups stage
musical, theatrical and dance performances. For a schedule and locations, call (408) 429-8433.

August

First Weekend. *Shakespeare/Santa Cruz Festival.* Month-long festival, at the Performing Arts Center, U.C. Santa Cruz. Conventional
performances of Shakespearean plays by professional theater organiza-
tions; outdoor theater settings. Also some workshops. Advance ticket
reservations recommended; (408) 429- 2121. *International Calamari*
Festival. Month-long celebration of the annual migration of the calamari
(squid) to Monterey Bay. Variety of entertainment, both at the Municipal Wharf and the India Joze Restaurant at 1001 Center St.; squid
inspired food. More information on (408) 427-3554.

Third Weekend. *Cabrillo Music Festival.* Held at U.C. Santa Cruz
and Cabrillo College, Aptos; 3rd and 4th weeks of the month. Outdoor
concerts in hilltop meadow, performed by nationally-known artists;
classical, jazz and pop music. Advance reservations advised. Call (408)
476-9064 or (408) 662-2701 for reservations and schedule.

September

First Weekend. *Loggers Day Festival.* Roaring Camp, Felton.
Popular annual event, featuring lumberjack competitions; also live entertainment, and food concessions. (408) 335-4484.

Second Weekend. *National Begonia Festival.* At the Capitola
Beach, in Capitola. Fun-filled event, with sand sculpture competition,
fishing derby and rowboat races, and a nautical parade in which bego-
nia-laden rafts race down the river toward the beach. For a program and
more information, call (408) 475-6522/476-3476. *Santa Cruz County*
Fair and Horse Show. Held at the Santa Cruz County Fairgrounds,
Watsonville. Events include a carnival, music, arts and crafts, refreshments, agricultural exhibits, and a wine competition. Also daily concert.
(408) 688-3384/(408) 724-3476. *Northern California Men's Beach Vol-*
leyball Tournament. Capitola Beach, Capitola. Several top teams from
Northern California compete for a variety of prizes. For a schedule, call
(408) 462-2365. *Capitola Art and Wine Festival.* Capitola Beach, Capi-

ola. Features 150 artists, free music and sidewalk entertainment, food stalls, and wine tasting featuring Monterey and Santa Cruz County wines. More information on (408) 475-6522.

October

First Weekend. *Watsonville Apple Butter Festival.* At Gizdich Ranch, 55 Packham Rd., Watsonville. Celebration of Watsonville's apple harvest; live music, food, games, and arts and crafts show, (408) 722-1056. *Oktoberfest.* In Aptos Village Park, Aptos. Features German bands, silent and oral auctions, and traditional German food. More information on (408) 688-1467.

Second Weekend. *Brussels Sprout Festival.* Held at the Santa Cruz Boardwalk. Celebration of the area's rich Brussels sprouts harvest. Sprouts prepared in every imaginable way, from sprout chip cookies and sprout soup, to deep-fried sprouts and sprout water taffy; also music and live entertainment. For festival information, call (408) 423-5590. *Harvest Faire.* At Roaring Camp, Felton; 2nd and 3rd weekends of the month. Demonstrations of 1880s crafts and special skills, including spinning, weaving, quilt-making and pumpkin carving; and scarecrow displays. Also, on Halloween, a ghost train travels through the ghost- and goblin-haunted redwood forest. (408) 335-4484. *Open Studios.* In Santa Cruz and Aptos, during the 2nd and 3rd weekends of the month. Self-guided tours of more than 300 artists' studios. (408) 688-5399. *Welcome Back Monarch's Day.* In Santa Cruz. Welcoming ceremonies for returning Monarch Butterflies. Home-spun music, poetry, humor, and skits; tours of the Monarchs' over-wintering site at Natural Bridges State Park. (408) 423-4609.

November

First Weekend. *Collector's Three.* At Santa Cruz County Fair Grounds, Watsonville. Arts and crafts fair, featuring works of local artists. (408) 688-3384.

Fourth Weekend. *Mountain Man Rendezvous.* At Roaring Camp, Felton. Demonstrations of 1830s and 1840s fur trappers and traders of the Old West, featuring axe throwing, black-powder musket displays, and native American Indian dances. (408) 335-4484. *Christmas Craft and Gift Festival.* Three-day festival, held at the Cocoanut Grove Ballroom, in a Victorian Christmas setting. Features 50 booths with crafts and gift items, holiday food and drink, live entertainment, and appearance by Santa Claus. (408) 423-5590.

December

First Weekend. *Pioneer Christmas.* Roaring Camp, Felton. Old-fashioned decorations, carollers, train rides, and treasure hunt in the redwood forest atop Bear Mountain. (408) 335-4484. *Winter Wonderland.* In Watsonville. Features an elaborate display of Christmas and winter scenes. (408) 728-6081.

PLACES OF INTEREST

Santa Cruz Beach Boardwalk. Situated along Santa Cruz Beach, at 400 Beach St., Santa Cruz. Coney Island-type amusement park, built in 1907 and claimed to be the only seaside amusement park on the West Coast. Features game arcades, refreshment stands, restaurants, gift and souvenir shops, a shooting gallery, and over 25 thrilling rides — including a half-mile-long roller coaster, the "Giant Dipper," built in 1924, with some 327,000 board-feet of lumber. Free admission; fee for individual rides. Open daily 11 a.m.-10 p.m. (11 a.m.-11 p.m. on Saturdays), May-Sept.; 12-5 weekends rest of the year. For more information, call (408) 426- RIDE/423-5590.

Cocoanut Grove Ballroom. Located adjacent to the Boardwalk, on Beach St., in Santa Cruz. Last remaining Victorian ballroom in Northern California, originally built in 1907. In 1981 the Cocoanut Grove was renovated at a cost of $10 million, and converted into a banquet and convention center. Now contains four unique rooms, including the glass-domed *Sun Room* which features a movable glass roof for open-air dining. The Cocoanut Grove still schedules big band concerts and other big name entertainment. For entertainment schedules and information, call (408) 423-2053/423-5590.

Joseph W. Long Marine Laboratory. Located at 100 Shaffer Rd., at the west end of Delaware Ave., near the Natural Bridges State Park, in Santa Cruz. Several marine exhibits on display, including an 85-foot-long skeleton of a blue whale. Also aquarium and tidal and petting pools on premises, open to public tours, Tues.-Sun. 1-4. The laboratory is part of the U.C. Santa Cruz facility. Phone (408) 459-2883.

Santa Cruz Municipal Wharf. Off Beach St., Santa Cruz. Colorful old wharf, lined with open-air fish markets, seafood restaurants and gift and souvenir shops. Originally built in 1914, and expanded in 1980 to accommodate pedestrian walkways and additional shops. A stage at the end of the wharf is used for weekend concerts. The wharf is also the site of the annual Calamari (Squid) Festival, held in August. Fishing charters available.

University of California, Santa Cruz. 1156 High St., Santa Cruz. Picturesque, 2,000-acre campus, with architect-designed buildings nestled among redwoods and other evergreens. Originally opened in 1966, the university is notable for its performing and visual arts programs. Campus maps for self-guided tours are available at the visitors information booth at the entrance. Information can also be obtained by calling the university on (408) 459-0111.

Mision la Exaltacion de la Santa Cruz. Situated on Mission Hill, at 126 High St., Santa Cruz. The Santa Cruz mission was the 12th of California's 21 Franciscan missions, founded by Father Junipero Serra in 1791. The present mission building is actually a half-size replica of the original mission, which was destroyed by fire in 1857; the replica dates from 1931. Small mission museum attached to main building, housing early-day mission relics, including books, vestments and other artifacts. Open daily 2-5.

Mission Hill. Oldest part of Santa Cruz, notable for its rich collection of "gingerbread" Victorians and other historic buildings, with a fair mber of them to be seen on High and Mission streets and Escalona rive.

Santa Cruz Surfing Museum. Located at Lighthouse Point, off 'est Cliff Dr., Santa Cruz. Superb collection of surfing memorabilia, cluding old surfing photographs, wooden surfboards, and on-going deo films on surfing. Open Thurs.- Mon., 12-4. Free admission; onations requested.

Santa Cruz Museum of Natural History. Located at the corner of ast Cliff Dr. and Pilkington Ave., Santa Cruz. Displays of native birds, ossils and Indian basketry, and a tidepool containing starfish and sea nemones. Open Tues.-Sat. 10-5, Sun. 12-5. Free admission; donations equested.

The Mystery Spot. 1953 Branciforte Dr., Santa Cruz; (408) 423-897. The "mystery spot" consists of a most unusual circle, measuring oughly 150 feet in diameter, in which balls roll uphill and trees grow ideways, completely defying the laws of gravity. This strange natural henomenon was first discovered in 1940. It is now open to public tours, .30-4:30 daily; admission: $3.00 adults, $1.50 children.

De Laveaga Park. Off Branciforte Dr., at the northeast end of Santa ruz; (408) 429-3777. Facilities include an 18-hole golf course, hiking nd horse trails, athletic fields, picnic area, restrooms, lodge and restaurant.

Harvey West Park. On Harvey West Blvd., just west from the ntersection of Hwys. 1 and 9, in Santa Cruz; (408) 429-3663. Swimming pool, athletic fields, rose garden, picnic and barbecue areas, children's playground.

San Lorenzo Park. 701 Ocean St., Santa Cruz. Grassy park with layground and duck pond. Site of outdoor concerts in summer. Day se. (408) 429-3663.

Wilder Ranch State Park. Located on Coast Rd., off Hwy. 1, 2 miles north of Santa Cruz. Theme park, centered around 19th-century dairy farm, with a collection of old, restored ranch buildings, including a farmhouse, a bunkhouse and workshop, a horse barn, and a Victorian mansion with original, period furnishings and decor. Also view exhibits of antique farm equipment, such as seed spreaders and road graders, and turn-of-the-century vehicles, among them a Model A Coupe and a 1916 Dodge Touring Sedan. Hiking trails; tours. Open 10-4 daily. Park phone, (408) 426-0505.

Ano Nuevo State Park. Situated on New Years Creek Rd., off Hwy. 1, 20 miles north of Santa Cruz. Undeveloped park, notable as a breeding ground for elephant seals — where more than 3,000 of these large marine mammals come ashore to mate and give birth to baby seals. Guided tours offered during breeding season, Dec.-Apr. Also tidepools, and whale-watching in season, usually in November. Open daily 9-3; admission $5.00 per car. Park phone, (415) 879-0595; for tour reservations, call (800) 444-7275.

Forest of Nisene Marks State Park. On Aptos Creek Rd., off Soquel Dr., 2 miles north of Aptos; (408) 335-4598. 10,000-acre park, containing remnants of an old Chinese labor camp. Also hiking trails through redwood forest, including one that leads to the epicenter of the October 17, 1989 earthquake that caused significant damage in Santa Cruz and San Francisco's Bay Area. Picnic facilities, and campground; camping fee: $3.00 per person.

Roaring Camp & Big Trees Railroad. Located on Graham Hill

Rd., at Felton. Recreated 1880s railroad camp, with original 19th-ce
tury steam locomotives offering rides through miles of redwood fore
The camp was originally founded in 1835, and named for its boistero
community; the railroad arrived some years later, in 1875. The camp
now open to the public daily, with several special old-time even
including chuck-wagon barbecues, country music, square dancing, ar
melodrama theater. Cost for train rides is $10.50 adults, $7.50 childre
For reservations and information, call (408) 335-4400/335-4484.

Big Basin Redwoods State Park. Situated along Hwy. 236, 9 mil
north of Hwy. 9, above Boulder Creek. This is California's oldest sta
reserve, originally founded in 1902. It encompasses nearly 16,000 acre
of redwood forest, with over 80 miles of hiking trails meanderir
through it. There is also a small nature museum here, with exhibits c
animals and plants of the region, and a 190-site, primitive campgroun
Ranger-led campfire programs in summer, featuring slide shows, mov
ies, and lectures. Day-use fee: $5.00 per car; camping fee: $14.00. Par
phone (408) 338-6132.

Castle Rock State Park. Located on Skyline Blvd. off Hwy. S
northeast of Big Basin Redwoods State Park; (408) 335- 9145/867
2952. Scenic, 4,000-acre park, with elevations ranging from 2,600 ft. t
3,200 ft.; named for the huge sandstone rock located in the park,
favorite of rock climbers. The park has over 43 miles of hiking an
backpacking trails, including part of the 24-mile Skyline to Sea Trail, a
well as a self-guided nature trail, 5 picnic sites, 2 primitive camp
grounds, and the spectacular Castle Rock Falls, plunging more than 10
feet.

Henry Cowell Redwoods State Park. Hwy. 9, just south of Felton
4,300-acre redwood park, containing several first-growth redwoods
some of them nearly 200 years old. Camping, picnicking, fishing an
swimming possibilities, and over 15 miles of hiking trails, including th
well-liked Redwood Grove Trail which loops through some of the mos
magnificent forest land. Park phone, (408) 335-4598; campground res
ervations, (800) 444-7275.

Highlands Park. 8500 Hwy. 9, Ben Lomond. Facilities include a
picnic area, playground, horseshoe pits, nature trails, volleyball court
and fishing in the San Lorenzo River.

Felton Covered Bridge. Located on Covered Bridge Road, off
Graham Hill Rd. (which goes off Hwy. 9), in Felton. One of California's
few remaining covered bridges, originally built in 1892, and now a State
Historical Landmark. The bridge is 140 feet long and 34 feet high
believed to be the tallest covered bridge of its kind in the country. Open
to foot traffic only.

Capitola Wharf. Historic 150-year-old wharf, now a designated
fishing pier, located at the end of Wharf Road. Nearby are the Capitola
Beach and the Esplanade, with several colorful little bars and restaurants. There is also a marina adjacent to the wharf, with fishing boat
rentals. Open year-round.

Antonelli Begonia Gardens. 2545 Capitola Rd., Capitola; (408)
475-5222. 6 acres of plants and tropical flowers, with an acre devoted to
begonias and fuschias alone. View gardens June-November for best
displays; peak season is Aug.-Sept. Free admission.

William H. Volck Museum. 261 E. Beach St., Watsonville; (408)
722-0305. Housed in the turn-of-the-century home of William H. Volck,
developer of modern pesticides and "savior of the apple industry" in the

jaro Valley. Features permanent and rotating displays of exhibits of
al historical interest, including a superb collection of costumes from
e late 1800s and early 1900s, and old photographs, dolls, ladies' glove
xes, and other such items. Small library and archive on premises.
useum hours: 11-3, Tues.-Thurs.

Also see *Santa Cruz Beaches*.

WINERIES

Santa Cruz Mountains

Bargetto Winery. 3535 North Main St., Soquel; (408) 475-2258.
ld family winery, established in 1933, overlooking Soquel Creek.
roduces varietal as well as fruit and berry wines. Gift shop and picnic
rea on premises. Tasting and sales, 11-5 daily.

Bonny Doon Vineyard. 10 Pine Flat Rd., Santa Cruz; (408) 425-
625/425-4518 (Tasting Room). Small Santa Cruz winery, owner-oper-
ted. Offers varietal Chardonnay and Claret from its 20-acre estate
ineyard. Picnic area on premises. Open for wine tasting and sales, 12-5
Ved.-Mon. (May-Sept.), 12-5 Fri.-Sun. (Oct.-Apr.); tours by appointment.

David Bruce Winery. 21439 Bear Creek Rd., Los Gatos; (408)
54-4214. Founded in 1964. Produces estate-grown Chardonnay and
inot Noir from its 28-acre vineyard located at the winery; also small
ots of Cabernet, Zinfandel, Gewurztraminer and Petite Sirah. Picnic
rea on premises. Tours, tasting and sales by appointment, Sat.-Sun.
2-5.

Crescini Wines. 2621 Old San Jose Rd., Soquel; (408) 462-1466.
wner-operated winery, offering three varietal wines — Cabernet Sau-
ignon, Merlot and Chenin Blanc. Picnic facilities. Tours, tasting and
ales on Saturdays, by appointment.

Devlin Wine Cellars. 3801 Park Ave., Soquel; (408) 476-7288.
0-acre wine estate, situated in the Santa Cruz Mountains, with views of
he ocean. Offers primarily varietal and sparkling wines. Tours, tasting
nd sales; picnic area. Open 12-5 on weekends.

Hallcrest Vineyards. 379 Felton Empire Rd., Felton; (408) 335-
4441. Located in the San Lorenzo Valley. Produces small lots of varietal
wines. Wine tasting and sales 11- 5.30 daily. Picnic area. **Roudon-
Smith Vineyards.** 2364 Bear Creek Rd., Santa Cruz; (408) 438-1244.
Producer of varietal wines, family owned and operated. Winery tours
and retail sales by appointment, Sat. 10-4.

Salamandre Wine Cellars. 108 Don Carlos Dr., Aptos; (408) 685-
0321. One of the area's newer wineries, producing varietal Chardonnay.
Winery visitors by appointment only.

Santa Cruz Mountain Vineyard. 2300 Jarvis Rd., Santa Cruz;
(408) 426-6209. Small, owner-operated winery, situated in the hills
above Santa Cruz. Produces estate-bottled Pinot Noir and Cabernet
Sauvignon from its 15-acre vineyard located at the winery. Picnic area.
Winery visits by appointment.

Storrs Winery. 303 Portrero St., Santa Cruz; (408) 458-5030.
Small, family owned and operated winery, producing varietal, vintage-

dated wines. Open for tasting and sales 12-5 Thurs.-Tues.; tours appointment.

Hecker Pass

A. Conrotto Winery. 1690 Hecker Pass Hwy.; (408) 842-305 Producer of table wines, established in 1933. Conrotto wines are so primarily to restaurants. Picnic area on premises. Tasting room open 9 daily.

Fortino Winery. 4525 Hecker Pass Hwy.; (408) 842- 3305. Owne operated winery, bottling a full line of varietal wines, some sparkli wine, and one or two proprietary and generic wines. Tours, tasting a sales; also picnic area and gift shop and deli on premises. Hours: 9 daily.

Hecker Pass Winery. 4605 Hecker Pass Hwy.; (408) 872- 875 Estate-bottled varietal wines; port, sherry. Picnic area overlooking vin yards. Winery and tasting room open daily, 10-5; tours by appointmer

Kirigin Cellars. 11550 Watsonville Rd., Gilroy; (408) 847-882 Newer winery, located on an old vineyard estate in the Uvas Valley the Hecker Pass district, originally established in 1916. Offers vintage dated, estate-bottled varietal wines, and small lots of sparkling wine ar a dessert wine, Vino de Mocca. Tasting room open 9-6 daily.

Live Oaks Winery. 3875 Hecker Pass Hwy., Gilroy; (408) 842 2401. One of the area's oldest wineries, founded in 1912. Produce premium Burgundy, Sauterne, Grenache Rosé, and Chablis. Large dis play of celebrity photographs; picnic area. Wine tasting and sales 8- daily.

Thomas Kruse Winery. 4390 Hecker Pass Hwy., Gilroy; (408 842-7016. Owner-operated winery, established in 1971. Offers vintage dated varietal wines and *méthode champenoise* sparkling wine. Tastin and sales 12-5 daily; tours by appointment. Picnic area.

Sarah's Vineyard. 4005 Hecker Pass Hwy., Gilroy; (408) 842 4278. Small producer of varietal wines. Visitors by appointment only.

Sycamore Creek Vineyards. 12775 Uvas Rd., Morgan Hill; (408 779-4738. Family owned and operated winery, established in 1976 o an historic vineyard estate dating from 1906. Estate-bottled, vintage dated varietal wines. Picnic area overlooking estate vineyard. Open fo tours, tasting and sales, Sat.-Sun. 11.30-5, weekdays by appointment.

RECREATION

Boating. Santa Cruz is a popular boating area, which also offer good fishing opportunities, and whale watching in season. Following are some of the area's charter and cruise boat operators, specializing ir fishing charters, moonlight cruises, whale watching excursions, and variety of boat cruises. *Tom's Fisherman's Supply*, 2210 E. Cliff Dr. Santa Cruz, (408) 476-2648; *Chardonnay Sailing Charters*, 1661 Pine Flat Rd., Santa Cruz, (408) 423-1213; *Pacific Yachting Unlimited*, 33: Lake St., Santa Cruz, (408) 476-2370; *Stagnaro Fishing Trips*, Munici

Wharf, Santa Cruz, (408) 425-7003; *Capitola Boat & Bait,* 1400
arf Rd., Capitola, (408) 462-2208; *Pleasure Point Charters,* 2-3665
Cliff Dr., Santa Cruz, (408) 475-4657.

Bicycling. *Dutchman Bicycles,* 3961 Portola Dr., Santa Cruz; (408)
5-9555. Bicycle rentals, sales and repairs; open daily. *Aptos Bike
ail,* 7514 Soquel Dr., Aptos; (408) 688-8650. Bicycle rentals and
airs; open daily (except Tues.). *Surf City Cycles,* 46 Front St., Santa
uz; (408) 423-9050. Rentals, sales and repairs.

Ballooning. *Gentle Adventure,* P.O. Box 1617, Morgan Hill, CA
038; (408) 778-1945. Offers hot-air balloon flights over the Morgan
ll-Gilroy Valley, originating in Morgan Hill. Champagne lunch.
ght cost: $145.00 per person. Reservations required.

Surfing. Santa Cruz is of course one of the most popular places for
rfing, on the California coast with scores of surf shops located there,
fering a variety of surfboards, boogie boards and wet-suits for both
ntal and sale, as well as surf and beach reports. Following are some of
e area surf shops, most of them located within a block or two of the
aches. *O'Neill's Surf Shop,* 1149 41st Ave., Capitola, (408) 475-4151,
d 2222 E. Cliff Dr., Santa Cruz, (408) 476-5200 (surf report on (408)
5-2275); *Arrow Surf and Sport,* 312 Capitola Ave., Capitola, (408)
5-8960, and 2322 Mission St., Santa Cruz, (408) 423-8286; *Full
eed,* 1040 41st Ave., Santa Cruz, (408) 479-7873; *Santa Cruz Surf
op,* 753 41st Ave., Santa Cruz, (408) 464-3233 (surf report on (408)
5-1616); *Freeline Design,* 861 41st Ave., Santa Cruz, (408) 476-
50.

Golf. For golf enthusiasts, the Santa Cruz area has several notable
urses to enjoy, among them — *DeLaveaga Golf Course,* Upper De
aveaga Dr., Santa Cruz, (408) 423-7212; *Pasatiempo Golf Course,*
ubhouse Rd. (off Hwy. 17), Santa Cruz, (408) 459-9155; *Aptos Sea-
ape Golf Course,* 610 Clubhouse Dr., Aptos, (408) 688-3213; *Boulder
reek Golf & Country Club,* Cnr. Hwys. 9 and 236, Boulder Creek,
08) 338-2121; *Pajaro Valley Golf Club,* 967 Salinas Rd., Watson-
lle, (408) 724-3851; *Spring Hills Golf Course,* 31 Smith Rd., Watson-
lle, (408) 724-1404; *Valley Gardens Golf Course,* 263 Mt. Hermon
d., Scotts Valley, (408) 438-3058.

Tennis. *Darby Park,* Woodland Way (next to Natural Bridges
chool), Santa Cruz; 2 courts, no lights. *Mike Fox Tennis Park,* cnr.
iverside Ave. and San Lorenzo Blvd., Santa Cruz; 4 courts, 2 lighted.
eary Lagoon Courts, cnr. Bay St. and California St., Santa Cruz; 3
urts plus 1 practice court. *Cabrillo College,* 6500 Soquel Dr., Aptos,
08) 479-6266; 9 courts, weekends only. *Highlands County Park,*
wy. 9, Ben Lomond; (408) 336-8551; 3 courts, no lights. *Jade Street
ark,* Cnr. Jade St. and 41st Ave., Capitola, (408) 475-5935; 4 courts,
ith lights.

SANTA CRUZ BEACHES

Santa Cruz Beach. Popular white sand beach, situated off Beach
treet, at the front of the Boardwalk. Swimming, surfing, sunbathing,
icnicking.

Natural Bridges Beach State Park. Situated at the end of W
Cliff Dr., near the Long Marine Laboratory. Well-liked rocky bea
named for its natural bridge-like rock formations. Excellent surf fish
and swimming possibilities; some picnicking. The park is also a go
place to see Monarch butterflies during their annual migration in Oc
ber. Open 8 a.m.-sunset; fee: $6.00 per car.

Cowell Beach. One of Santa Cruz' best-loved beaches, situa
adjacent to the Boardwalk. Volleyball courts, lifeguards in summ
swimming and sunbathing. Close to shops and restaurants.

Lighthouse Point. West Cliff Dr. Site of the Santa Cruz Surfi
Museum. Spectacular views; a great spot to watch surfers tackle t
infamous Steamers Lane.

San Lorenzo Point/Castles Beach. Long, sandy beach, situated
East Cliff Dr., between the San Lorenzo River cove and the Santa Cr
Yacht Harbor. Lifeguards in summer; hot dog stands; restrooms.

Pleasure Point. Situated along East Cliff Dr., at 41st Ave., wi
rocky paths leading down to the beach. Well-known surfing spot.

Moran Lake Beach. Popular surfing beach, located off East Cl
Dr., at 26th Ave.

Sunny Cove. At the end of 17th Ave., off East Cliff Dr. Favori
haunt of bodysurfers.

Lincoln Beach. Quiet, sandy beach at the end of 12th Ave., with
stairway leading down to the beach. No facilities.

Twin Lakes Beach State Park. Situated along East Cliff Dr., ea
of the Yacht Harbor. Well-liked bonfire beach; features two lagoon
one of which is a wildfowl refuge and the other an 850-berth small-cra
harbor. Picnic facilities; fire pits.

Capitola Beach. Located at the seaside resort of Capitola, along tł
Esplanade, some 3 miles south of Santa Cruz. Lovely, sheltered beac
with a freshwater lagoon and beachfront restaurants and bars. Pi
fishing; and river rafting down the Soquel Creek.

New Brighton State Park. Just south of Capitola, off Hwy.
Popular sandy beach and picnic area, with overnight camping facilitie

Seacliff State Beach. Located along Santa Cruz Ave., south
Capitola and the New Brighton State Park, off Hwy. 1, at Aptos; (40
688-3222. Camping and picnicking; also good pier fishing from tł
unique Seacliff pier, which is actually made up of a 435-foot-lon
vintage cement ship, the Palo Alto.

Red, White & Blue Beach. 6 miles north of Santa Cruz, off Hwy.
(408) 423-6332. Swimsuits-optional beach, with volleyball and tethe
ball courts, picnic facilities, and hot showers. Camping available. A
mission: $5.00.

Sunset State Beach. Situated along Sunset Beach Rd., near Hwy.
and San Andreas Rd., 16 miles south of Santa Cruz; (408) 724
1266/688-3241. Popular surfing and swimming beach. Campground
fishing, picnicking. Handicapped facilities.

Manresa State Beach. 13 miles south of Santa Cruz, off San An
dreas Rd. Day use beach, with good surfing possibilities.

CAMPGROUNDS

Mount Madonna County Park. Between Watsonville and Gilroy Hecker Pass Rd. (Hwy. 152); (408) 842-2341. 117 campsites and RV ces, piped water, restrooms, and picnicking and hiking. Campground ated at 1300-foot elevation. Camping fee: $8.00.

Monterey Vacation. 1400 Hwy. 101, Aromas; (408) 757-8098. 88 spaces with full hookups; flush toilets, showers, a swimming pool, zzi, laundry, propane gas, recreation room with square dancing, and tting green. Camping fee: $18.00.

Big Basin Redwoods State Park. 21600 Big Basin Way, Boulder ek; (408) 338-6132/(800) 444-7275. 188 spaces for 27-foot RVs and foot trailers; also walk-in and drive-in campsites, water, fireplaces picnic tables at each site. Showers, restrooms, water, picnic tables, places, and a store and dump station. 80 miles of hiking trails. ndicapped facilities. Camping fee: $14.00. Reservations suggested.

Sunset State Beach. 201 Sunset Beach Rd., Watsonville; (408) -1266. Beachfront campground, with 90 campsites and RV spaces; ilities include restrooms, hot showers, picnic tables, fireplaces, and a reation room. Camping fee: $16.00. Reservations suggested Mar.- t.

Forest of Nisene Marks State Park, West Ridge Trail Camp. 101 rth Big Trees Park Rd., Felton; (408) 335-4598/(800) 444-7275. 6 mitive campsites located 3 miles inside park. Outhouses. Camping : $3.00 per person per night. Reservations required.

Henry Cowell Redwoods State Park. Graham Hill Rd., Felton; 8) 335-4598/438-2396/(800) 444-7275. 112 campsites and spaces 35-foot RVs and 27-foot trailers; also picnic tables, fire rings, water, wers, toilets, a dump station, and several miles of hiking trails. ndicapped facilities. Camping fee: $16.00. Reservations suggested.

New Brighton State Beach. 1500 Park Ave., Hwy. 1, Capitola; 8) 475-4850/(800) 444-7275. 105 spaces for 31-foot RVs and trail- , without hookups; also 10 campsites, picnic tables, fireplaces, water, wers, toilets, dump stations, propane gas, a store and laundry. Camp- fee: $16.00. Reservations recommended.

Seacliff State Beach. State Park Dr., Aptos; (408) 688- 3222/688- 41/(800) 444-7275. Beachfront campground with 91 spaces for 36- t trailers and 40-foot RVs. Picnic tables, fireplaces, showers, store, pane gas, and laundry. Camping fee: $25.00. Reservations recom- nded.

Beach RV Park. 2505 Portola Dr., Santa Cruz; (408) 462-2505. cilities include full hookups, and picnic area and barbecue pits. Close beach. Camping fee: $15.00-$22.00. Reservations recommended.

Carbonera Creek RV Park. 917 Disc Dr., (off Scotts Valley Rd.), otts Valley; (408) 438-1288. 10 campsites, 116 spaces for RVs and ilers, with full hookups; also restrooms, showers, swimming pool, a, recreation room and laundry, and picnic facilities. Leashed pets owed. Reservations suggested. Camping fee: $18.50-$22.00.

Cotillion Gardens. 300 Old Big Trees Rd., Felton; (408) 335-7669. campsites and spaces with full hookups for RVs and trailers, strooms, showers, picnic tables, fireplaces, store, pool, and recreation hall. Campground adjoins Henry Cowell State Park. Camping $24.00-$26.00. Reservations recommended.

Redwood Rest Resort. 150 E. Grove, Boulder Creek; (408) 3413. 20 campsites, 20 spaces with full hookups for 40-foot RVs trailers; other facilities include showers, restrooms, picnic tables barbecue pits, a playground and heated pool. Wooded setting. O May-Oct. Camping fee: $18.00.

KOA Kampgrounds of America. 1186 San Andreas Rd. (off F 1), Watsonville; (408) 722-0551/722-2377. 233 spaces for RVs trailers with full hookups, 20 campsites, restrooms, showers, pi water, picnic tables, fireplaces, propane gas, swimming pool, st recreation room, laundry, and dump station. Camping fee: $21. $25.00. Open all year; reservations suggested.

Loma Linda RV Park. 890 Salinas Rd., Watsonville; (408) 7 9311. 54 spaces with full hookups, restrooms, showers, dump stati propane gas, and picnic tables. Handicapped facilities. Camping $15.00-$20.00. Open year-round; reservations suggested.

Marmo's Pinto Lake. 324 Amesti Rd., Watsonville; (408) 7 4533. 50 campsites with water and electrical hookups, picnic tables, rings, barbecue pits, hot showers, restrooms, store, and fishing in Pi Lake. Camping fee: $15.00.

Pinto Lake Park. 451 Green Valley Rd., Watsonville; (408) 7. 8129. 80-acre campground with spaces for RVs and trailers with hookups; restrooms, picnicking, fishing, sailing, and boat rent Camping fee: $15.00.

Santa Vida Trailer Park. 1611 Branciforte Dr., Santa Cruz (3 mi east of Santa Cruz); (408) 425-1945. 47 spaces for 32-foot RVs, so with full hookups; also campsites, showers, playground, swimm pool, picnic tables, fireplaces, and hiking trails. Camping fee: $14. $24.00.

Seacliff Center Trailer Park. 234 State Park Dr., Seacliff; (4(688-3813. Smaller campground, with 33 spaces, including 25 spa with full hookups, TV and phones, and picnic tables; other facilit include restrooms, showers, laundry, and a nearby store. Located n the Seacliff State Park. Camping fee: $20.00 a night, $120.00 a we $310.00 a month. Reservations suggested.

Smithwoods RV Park. 4770 Hwy. 9, Felton; (408) 335-4321. 1 spaces for RVs and trailers, with full hookups; also picnic tabl fireplaces, showers, restrooms, pool, recreation room, playground, lau dromat, and small store. The campground is nestled amid redwoo near Roaring Camp. Camping fee: $24.00.

Castle Rock State Park. On Skyline Blvd., off Hwy. 9, northeast Big Basin Redwoods State Park; (408) 338-6132/335-9145/867-29! Offers two primitive campgrounds: the Castle Rock campground has campsites, with picnic tables, water, fire rings and pit toilets; the Wate man Gap campground, reached by way of a 12-15 mile hike, has wat and pit toilets. Camping fee: $3.00 per person per night. Reservatio required for the Waterman Gap campground.

RESTAURANTS

Restaurants prices — based on full course dinner, excluding drinks, tax and tips — are categorized as ollows: Deluxe, over $30; Expensive, $20-$30; Moderate, $10-$20; Inexpensive, under $10.)

Santa Cruz

Acapulco Beachcomber. *Moderate-Expensive.* 533 Ocean St.; 408) 429-1407. Steaks, seafood, ribs, and a wide selection of Mexican dishes, including fajitas, burritos and chimichangas. Open for lunch and dinner daily, brunch on weekends.

Adolph's. *Moderate.* 525 Water St.; (408) 423-4403. Family- style Italian restaurant, specializing in pasta dinners; also seafood, steaks, and prime rib. Open for lunch and dinner; brunch on Sundays.

Aldos Restaurant. *Moderate.* Located at the Santa Cruz Yacht Harbor, at 616 Atlantic Ave; (408) 426-3736. Homemade ravioli and Italian fugasa bread, and fresh seafood. Open for breakfast and lunch daily

Anna Maria's Italian Restaurant. *Moderate.* 640 Eaton St.; (408) 475-5535. Homemade Italian dishes, and light seafood lunches. Favorites here are Fettucini Alfredo and Italian Wedding Soup; also live Maine Lobster. Open for dinner Wed.-Sun.

Bamboo Restaurant. *Inexpensive.* 1733 Seabright Ave; (408) 426-6382. Traditional family-style Chinese meals, featuring authentic Cantonese and Szechuan cooking, including steamed rockeye. Lunch and dinner Tues.-Sun.

Bocci's Cellar. *Moderate.* 140 Encinal St.; (408) 427-1795. Specializing in Continental and Italian cuisine; steak lobster, prime rib, and pasta. Cocktail lounge, and outdoor patio. Open for lunch Mon.-Fri., dinner daily.

Casablanca Restaurant. *Expensive-Moderate.* Cnr. Beach and Main Sts.; (408) 426-9063. Continental cuisine, featuring fresh seafood, steaks and homemade desserts. Extensive wine list. Also Sunday Brunch, comprising seafood, quiche and egg dishes. Dinners from 5 p.m. daily.

China Szechwan Restaurant. *Inexpensive.* 221 Cathcart St.; (408) 423-1178. Authentic Szechwan cuisine; informal atmosphere. Open for lunch and dinner, 11-3 and 5-9.30, Tues.-Sun.

The Cocoanut Grove Sun Room. *Inexpensive-Moderate.* 400 Beach St.; (408) 423-2053/423-5590. Sunday Champagne Brunch, 9.30-1.30; omelettes, freshly baked blueberry muffins, and other pastries. The Sun Room also features a 4,000-square-foot glass roof which can be retracted for open-air dining. Superb views of the beach and bay.

The Crow's Nest. *Moderate-Expensive.* Located at the Santa Cruz Yacht Harbor; (408) 476-4560. Waterfront setting; superb views. House specialties include salmon filet and fresh grilled sole with butter sauce; also steaks, and gourmet salad bar. Lunch and dinner daily; brunch on Sundays.

Dolphin Restaurant. *Moderate.* Municipal Wharf; (408) 426-5830. Wharfside setting; ocean views. Offers primarily American fare, including burgers, sandwiches, and lobster and crab. Breakfast, lunch and dinner daily.

El Paisano. *Moderate.* 605 Beach St; (408) 426-2382. Traditiona Mexican food, including burritos and tamales. Garden patio. Open fc breakfast, lunch and dinner.

El Palomar. *Inexpensive-Moderate.* 1136 Pacific Garden Mal (408) 425-7575. Mexican-seafood restaurant; features daily special including several vegetarian and chili dishes. Multi-flavored margaritas Mariachis on Friday and Sunday nights. Open for lunch and dinner.

Front Street Pub-Santa Cruz Brewing Co. *Moderate.* 516 Fron St.; (408) 429-8838. Casual, pub-style restaurant, featuring salads sandwiches, and fish and chips. Front Street is also notable as Sant Cruz's first microbrewery, producer of Lighthouse Lager. Open fo lunch and dinner daily.

Gilda's. *Inexpensive-Moderate.* Located at the Municipal Wharf (408) 423-2010. Casual wharfside restaurant, offering fish, steak, prim rib, sandwiches, soups, and salads; also cocktails. Open 6.30 a.m.-9.3(p.m. daily.

Hindquarter Bar & Grille. *Moderate-Expensive.* 303 Soquel Ave. (408) 426-7770. Fresh Monterey Bay seafood, poultry, steaks, laml chops, prime rib, and pasta. Patio for outdoor dining. Open for lunch Mon.-Fri., dinner daily.

Hungry Pelican. *Moderate-Expensive.* Municipal Wharf; (408) 458-3550. Waterfront setting, with superb views of the bay. Specializ ing in fresh seafood, pasta, and chicken; also sandwiches and soups. Open for lunch and dinner Tues.-Sun., breakfast on weekends. Reserva tions recommended.

Ideal Fish Restaurant. *Moderate-Expensive.* 106 Beach St. (408) 423-5271. Seafood menu, featuring Bouillabaisse, Cioppino, Linguini Calabrese, Monterey Bay Sandabs, and King Salmon. Open for dinner.

India Joze Restaurant. *Moderate-Expensive.* 1001 Center St.; (408) 427-3554. Home of the International Calamari Festival. Wide selection of exotic foods, including Middle Eastern, East Indian, Indo- nesian and Asian. Delicious baked desserts. Open for breakfast Mon.- Fri., lunch and dinner daily, also Sunday brunch, 10-2.30.

The Library at Chaminade Whitney. *Expensive.* One Chaminade Lane; (408) 475-5600. Elegant restaurant, housed in the historic Chaminade Monastery complex which has undergone a $17-million trans- formation into a corporate meeting place and retreat. Spectacular views of Santa Cruz; Continental cuisine. Open for dinner, and Sunday brunch.

Pearl Alley Bistro. *Moderate-Expensive.* 110 Pearl Alley (between Pacific and Cedar Sts.); (408) 429-8070. Features ethnic cuisine from Japan, France and Italy. Menu changes daily. Dinner Tues.-Sun. Reser- vations suggested.

Polivios. *Moderate.* Cnr. 15th Ave. and East Cliff Dr.; (408) 475- 7600. Continental cuisine, including prime rib, steak, veal, spaghetti, ravioli, prawns, and hot and cold sandwiches. Live music on weekends. Open daily for breakfast, lunch and dinner.

Royal Taj. *Moderate.* 270 Soquel Ave.; (408) 427-2400. Authentic Indian cuisine. Open for lunch and dinner daily.

Sea Cloud. *Moderate-Expensive.* Municipal Wharf; (408) 458-9393. Menu stresses fresh seafood and nouvelle cuisine sauces. Nautical at- mosphere; overlooking the Boardwalk and Steamers Lane. Open for lunch and dinner.

Stagnaro Brothers. *Moderate.* At the end of the Wharf; (408) 423-2180. Fresh seafood specialties, including calamari, seafood ouies, clam chowder, and live crabs and lobster. Casual atmosphere; weeping ocean views. Lunch and dinner daily.

Sukeroku. *Moderate.* 1701 Mission St.; (408) 426-6660. Japanese estaurant, serving Nigiri, Hosumaki, and Sashimi; also Sushi Bar. Open or lunch Wed.-Fri., dinner Tues.- Sun.

The Swan/Heavenly Goose. *Moderate.* Located in the Santa Cruz lotel, at 1003 Cedar St.; (408) 425-8988/426-2994. One of Santa Cruz' ldest Chinese restaurants, specializing in Szechuan cuisine. Cocktail ar. Dinners from 5 p.m.

Tampico Kitchen. *Inexpensive-Moderate.* 822 Pacific Ave.; (408) :58-2821. Informal Mexican restaurant. Late night dining; Mariachis on undays. Open for lunch and dinner.

Twelve Winds Restaurant. *Moderate-Expensive.* At the Dream nn, 175 W. Cliff Dr.; (408) 423-5732. Polynesian restaurant, specializ-ng in steak, seafood and chicken preparations; seafood buffet on Fri-ays. Live entertainment; ocean views. Dinners from 4.30 p.m. daily; reakfast on weekends.

San Lorenzo Valley

Adelita's Mexican. *Inexpensive-Moderate.* 13271 Hwy. 9, Boulder Creek; (408) 338-2632. Authentic Mexican cooking. Menu features, chicken and beef dishes, and whole red snapper. Redwood-shaded patio for outdoor dining. Open for lunch and dinner daily, breakfast on weekends.

AOI Restaurant. *Moderate.* 4727 Scotts Valley; (408) 438-1155. Japanese restaurant, specializing in tempura and teriyaki. Lunch 11.30-1.30 Tues.-Fri., dinner 5.30-9.30 Tues.- Sun.

Backstage. *Inexpensive.* 226A Mount Hermon Rd., Scotts Valley; (408) 438-0606. Burgers, chili, and clam chowder. Open 11 a.m.-8:30 p.m. Mon.-Sat.

Boulder Brewing Co. and Restaurant. *Inexpensive-Moderate.* 13040 Hwy. 9, Boulder Creek; (408) 338-7882. Menu features pasta, vegetarian and beef dishes primarily. Also locally-brewed beer. Open for lunch and dinner Wed.-Sun.

The Gathering Place. *Inexpensive-Moderate.* 9341 Mill, Ben Lo-mond; (408) 336-8818. English cafe atmosphere. Light gourmet fare, including quiche, lasagna, stuffed croissants, and ice cream desserts; also espresso bar and gourmet coffees. Entertainment on weekends; displays of work of local artists. Open for breakfast, lunch and dinner.

Hooked on Fish. *Moderate.* 11 Camp Eyers Ln., Scotts Valley; (408) 438-0522. Casual seafood cafe, serving locally-caught, char-broiled fish, as well as fish and chips, and pasta. Open for lunch and dinner, Tues.-Sat.

Mama Mia's. *Moderate-Expensive.* 6231 Graham Hill Rd., Felton; (408) 335-4414. Homemade pasta and pizza, and seafood, and veal and poultry entrees. Dinner daily; brunch on Sundays.

Mei Garden Chinese Restaurant. *Inexpensive-Moderate.* 4303½ Scotts Valley Dr., Scotts Valley; (408) 438-5772. Hunan and Szechuan dishes. Open for lunch and dinner daily; buffet brunch on weekends.

New Peking Restaurant. *Moderate.* 13375 Hwy. 9, Boulder Creek; (408) 338-7258. Specializing in Szechuan and Mandarin cuisine. Patio for outdoor dining. Open for dinner daily.

Old Mountain Inn. *Inexpensive.* 13132 Central Ave., Bould
Creek; (408) 338-2211. Variety of omelettes and pancakes, soups, san
wiches, burgers. Open for breakfast and lunch, Fri.-Tues.

Squisi's Ristorante Italiano. *Expensive.* 9217 Hwy. 9, Bould
Creek; (408) 336-2006. Traditional Italian cuisine. Extensive wine li
Dinner Wed.-Sun.; Sunday brunch. Reservations recommended.

Tampico Grande. *Inexpensive.* 6275 Hwy. 9, Felton; (408) 33
9137. Authentic Mexican cooking. Open for lunch and dinner daily.

Tyrolean Inn. *Expensive.* 9600 Hwy. 9, Ben Lomond; (408) 33
5188. Continental cuisine. Lunch and dinner Tues.-Sun.

Capitola, Soquel and Aptos

Antoine's Inn. *Moderate.* 200 Monterey Ave., Capitola; (408) 47
1974. Authentic Cajun-Creole cooking, featuring coconut beer-batte
prawns, duck and crab gumbo, jambalaya, and blackened filet migno
Also some pasta dishes. Live blues piano; wine bar. Dinners from
p.m., Tues.-Sun.

Aragona's. *Moderate-Expensive.* 2591 Main St., Soquel; (408) 462
5100. Traditional Italian cuisine. Several old family recipes, and home
made gelato and cannoli. Open for dinner daily.

Balzac Bistro. *Moderate-Expensive.* 112 Capitola Ave., Capitola
(408) 476-5035. European restaurant, featuring pasta, seafood and sa
ads. Extensive wine list. Dinner daily; brunch on weekends, 10-4
Reservations recommended.

Cafe Sparrow. *Moderate-Expensive.* 8042 Soquel Dr., Aptos; (408
688-6238. French country cuisine, emphasizing fresh fruits and vegeta
bles. Specialties include classic Caesar salad, and grilled chicken cov
ered with brie. Open for breakfast, lunch and dinner Tues.-Sun., brunc
on weekends.

Cafe Rio. *Moderate-Expensive.* 131 Esplanade, Rio del Mar (jus
south of Aptos); (408) 688-8917. Fresh seafood; also oyster bar. Lunc
Mon.-Fri., dinner daily from 5 p.m.; reservations recommended.

Chez Renee. *Expensive.* 9051 Soquel Dr., Aptos; (408) 688-5566
Award-winning restaurant, featuring California cuisine with an Italia
flavor. Patio for outdoor dining. Open for lunch Tues.-Fri., dinne
Tues.-Sat.

Country Court Tearoom. *Moderate.* 911B Capitola Ave., Capitola
(408) 462-2498. Intimate dining rooms, and courtyard. Popovers
poached eggs with creole sauce, corn muffins, winter root soup wit
sour cream and dill, quiche, homemade desserts and ice cream; als
champagne brunch. Breakfast Mon.-Fri., lunch daily 11.30-3 p.m., an
brunch on weekends.

Deer Park Tavern. *Expensive.* 783 Rio Del Mar Blvd., Rio De
Mar; (408) 688-5800. Historic restaurant, established in 1937. Special
izing in seafood and aged beef. Live entertainment and dancing. Lunc
11-2.30, dinner 5-9 p.m. Mon.-Fri., to 10 p.m. weekends.

El Puentito. *Inexpensive-Moderate.* 316 Capitola Ave., Capitola
(408) 475-4330. Mexican food, including tamales, chili verde, fajitas
seafood and flan. Open 12 noon-10 p.m. daily.

Golden Buddha. *Moderate.* 4610 Soquel Dr., Soquel; (408) 479

788. Specializing in Szechuan cuisine. Lunch and dinner daily.

Good Golly Miss Lolly's. *Inexpensive-Moderate.* 10110 Soquel Ave., (cnr. Freedom Blvd. and Hwy. 1), Aptos; (408) 688-6839. A local favorite, serving Mexican and American fare, including prime rib, baked ham, and oven-roasted turkey with all the trimmings. Open 6 a.m.-9 p.m. daily.

Margaritaville. *Inexpensive-Moderate.* 221 Esplanade, Capitola; (408) 476-2263. Splendid setting, at the Capitola Beach. Enormously popular Mexican restaurant. Exotic drinks, and multi-flavored Margaritas. Open daily 11.30 a.m.-1 a.m.

Paiolo's. *Moderate.* 7960 Soquel Dr., Aptos; (408) 688-3262. Family-style Italian restaurant. Lunch Mon.-Fri., dinner Wed.-Sun.

Palapas. *Moderate.* 21 Seascape Village, Aptos; (408) 662-9000. Mexican seafood, fish, tacos and vegetarian dishes. Modern Mexican decor; views of Monterey Bay and ravine. Open for lunch 11-2.30, dinner from 5 p.m.

Panda Inn. *Moderate.* 5 Deer Park Center, Cnr. Hwy. 1 and Rio del Mar, Aptos; (408) 688-8620. Traditional Northern Chinese cooking, with emphasis on Mandarin and Szechuan specialties. California wines. Open for lunch and dinner daily. Reservations suggested.

Ranjeet's. *Moderate.* 3051 Porter Rd., Soquel; (408) 475-6407. Continental cuisine. Specialties include Salmon Wellington, Scampi Prawns, and Chicken Madagascar in brandy. Santa Cruz wines. Dinners from 5:30 daily.

Ristorante Italiano. *Moderate-Expensive.* 555 Soquel Dr., Soquel; (408) 458-2321. Regional Italian cuisine and pasta specialties; extensive selection of Italian wines. Open for lunch Mon.-Fri., dinner daily.

Severino's Restaurant. *Expensive.* At the Seacliff Inn, 7500 Old Dominion Court, Aptos; (408) 688-8987. Elegant restaurant, overlooking koi pond and waterfall. Features seafood, steaks, chicken and pasta. Open for breakfast, lunch and dinner; brunch on Sundays. Dinner reservations recommended.

Shadowbrook Restaurant. *Expensive.* 1750 Wharf Rd., Capitola; (408) 475-1511. Fresh seafood, scampi and prime rib. Dinner daily, lunch on weekends. Reservations recommended.

Star of Siam. *Moderate.* 3005 Porter St., Soquel; (408) 479-0366. Authentic Thai cuisine. Specialties include shrimp, chicken, squid, and fish; also sushi bar. Good selection of Asian beer and wine, and saki. Open for lunch 11.30-2.30 Mon.-Fri.; dinner 5 p.m.-9.30 p.m. daily.

The Veranda. *Expensive.* At the Bayview Hotel, 8041 Soquel Dr., Aptos; (408) 685-1881. Seasonal menu, emphasizing new American and California cuisine. Patio dining. Open for lunch Mon.-Fri., dinner daily.

Zelda's. *Moderate.* 203 Esplanade, Capitola; (408) 475-4900. Casual restaurant and club, featuring Continental cuisine, including seafood, pasta, chicken, steak, broiled mahi mahi, and calamari; full bar. Beachside setting, with view of the Capitola Wharf. Lunch and dinner daily; Sunday brunch.

Watsonville

Bamboo Garden. *Inexpensive-Moderate.* 1012 East Lake Ave.; (408) 724-1486. Cantonese cuisine. Open for lunch and dinner, Wed.-Mon.

Cilantros. *Moderate.* 1934 Main St.; (408) 761-2161. Tradition. Mexican fare, featuring handmade corn tortillas and homemade sals: and sauces; also vegetarian specialties, charbroiled prawns, broile snapper, and marinated steak. Voted "Best Burrito" at the Watsonvil: Burrito Bash Festival. Open for lunch and dinner daily, and Sunda brunch.

Del Monte Cafe. *Inexpensive-Moderate.* 300 Walker St. (nea Beach St.); (408) 724-2161. Casual cafe, established in 1910. Feature traditional American fare, such as steaks, pork chops, sandwiches an burgers, chicken, and seafood; full bar. Open for lunch 11-2 Mon.-Fri dinner 5-9 p.m. Mon.-Sat.

Lorene's Packing Shed. *Moderate-Expensive.* 972 Main St; (408 722-2566. American cuisine. Menu features steaks, fish, barbecue specialties, and salads; also cocktails. Open for lunch and dinner daily

Miramar of Watsonville. *Moderate-Expensive.* 526 Main St.; (408 724-5153. Family-style restaurant. Fresh seafood and pasta dishes Open for lunch and dinner daily.

Mt. Madonna Inn. *Moderate.* 1285 Hecker Pass Rd; (408) 724 2275. Situated in the Hecker Pass area at an elevation of 1,300 feet overlooking valley towns. Serves primarily Continental dishes, includ ing prime rib, filet mignon, pepper steak, veal parmigiana, veal cordo bleu, pastas, seafood, and chicken; good selection of local wines. Ope Thurs.-Sun. 5-10 p.m.; Sunday brunch 10 a.m.-3 p.m.

Miyuki. *Moderate.* 452 East Lake Ave.; (408) 728-1620. Japanese cuisine, featuring tempura, sashimi, teriyaki, and sukiyaki. Asian bee and wine; also saki. Open for lunch Tues.-Fri. 11-2, dinner Tues.-Sun 5-9 p.m.; Sunday buffet.

Zuniga's. *Inexpensive-Moderate.* 100 Aviation Way; (408) 724 5788. Oldest Mexican restaurant in the Monterey Bay area, offering homestyle Mexican food. Open for lunch and dinner daily.

THE GAME OF GOLF

Golf is a game of distance and direction, in which the objective is to drive the ball from one given point to another—from the tee-off point to the green and into the hole—in the least number of strokes. Each hole has a prescribed number of strokes—known as *Par*—in which it must be completed. One stroke over *Par* is known as a *Bogey*; one under *Par* is a *Birdie*, and two under *Par*, an *Eagle*.

The basic equipment required to play golf is the essential golf set, which comprises, besides golf balls and tees, golf clubs, made up of irons and woods—the latter used almost exclusively for beginning a round, or "teeing off"—as well as a wedge and a putter. The woods and irons are numbered, 1 through 9; the smaller the number, the greater the driving potential. Thus, a Number 1 wood, for instance, has the potential to drive a ball farther, to achieve greater distance, than, say, a Number 6 iron. A wedge is used to lift a ball upwards, primarily out of trouble spots, such as sand bunkers; while a putter is used, once on the green, to putt the ball into the hole.

The game of golf also requires technique. The basic technique has primarily three components—grip, stance, and swing.

The Grip

A good stroke begins with a good grip. The grip, ideally, must be snug yet firm, with perfect hand alignment. Typically, only five fingers grip the club—the last three fingers of the left hand and the middle two of the right hand—with the other fingers and thumbs simply settling in their correct positions on the shaft.

Begin by placing the club in the correct position, with the sole of the club flat on the ground and its face square to the target. Then grip the shaft in your left hand, such that it settles comfortably in the crease between the palm and last three fingers of the hand. The forefinger can then be positioned alongside the other fingers, and the thumb on the upperside of the shaft, pointing directly down.

Next, fit the middle two fingers of the right hand directly below the left hand, such that the right ring finger is snugly against the left forefinger, with the right little finger lying in the groove of the first and second fingers of the left hand. Then, again, settle the right forefinger comfortably alongside the middle two fingers of that hand, and the right thumb on the upperside of the shaft, pointing downward.

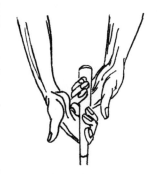

Grip

The Stance

A correct stance is equally important, and fundamental to good golf. The stance, quite typically, must be comfortable, with the legs apart (approximately the width of the player's shoulders), a slight bend or flexibility in the knees, back straight, weight well back on the heels, and feet firmly on the ground. When driving with a wood or iron, the feet must be on either side of the ball, such that the ball is slightly forward of center, directly in front of the player; when putting, the leading foot must be in line with the ball, at an approximate right angle to the intended stroke. In either case, it is important that one does not overreach to strike the ball. It is also important, when assuming the correct stance, to line up the play by looking from the target to the ball, rather than from the ball to the target.

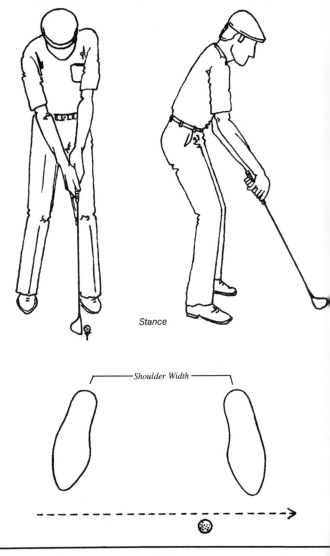

Stance

Shoulder Width

The Swing

Finally, it is the swing that determines the distance and direction of the ball. The swing, primarily, comprises four parts—backswing, downswing, impact, and follow-through.

Backswing. A good way to begin a backswing from address is with a "forward press," which, quite simply, gets the body moving and presses the wrists forward, cocking them. From the forward press position, simply straighten back to the original position and continue on back into a smooth backswing, with the left arm straight, wrists still cocked, right elbow bending, hips and knees turning into the swing, head stationary, and eyes—always—on the ball. At the top of the backswing, ideally, the clubhead should be high above the head, the left shoulder pressed hard against the chin, the right elbow bent and close to the ribs, and the left knee slightly angled into the swing.

Downswing. The downswing starts at the top of the backswing, and ends upon impact, or contact between the clubhead and the ball. Begin by turning the hips and knees into the downswing, and let the straight left arm pull the club toward the ball. Well into the swing, as you approach the ball, straighten out the right elbow, uncocking the wrists just before impact, such that the face of the club strikes the ball exactly square. It is important, all through the swing, to keep your head steady, and eyes on the ball. It is also equally important to not let the shoulders come around into the swing before the hips and the knees.

Impact. Impact occurs at the bottom of the downswing, when you hit the ball; and if the backswing and downswing have been perfectly executed, the face of the club should encounter the ball absolutely square, resulting in the perfect shot.

Follow-through. The follow-through is simply a continuation of the swing forward, through the impact, and should trace the same smooth arc as the swing.

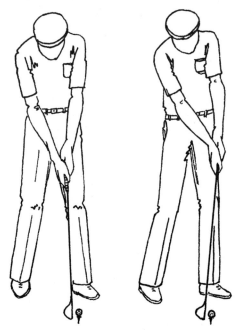

The Forward Press

Backswing

Downswing

Downswing Momentum

INDEX

The abbreviation MP stands for Monterey Peninsula.
The abbreviation SC stands for Santa Cruz.

Accommodations, MP
  55-63, SC 111-114
Allen Knight Maritime
  Museum, 20, 70
Alvarado Adobe, 80-81
American Tin Cannery, 26,
  71
Andrew Molera State Park,
  45, 73
Ano Nuevo State Park, 121
Antonelli Begonia Gardens,
  122
Aptos, 108, *map*, 97
Artichoke Festival, 53, 68
Asilomar Conference
  Center, 30
Asilomar State Beach, 70

Ballooning, MP 86, SC 125
Barnyard, The, 39, 73
Basilica San Carlos
  Borromeo del Rio
  Carmelo, *see* Carmel
  Mission
Beaches, SC 125-126
Bed & Breakfast Inns, MP
  63-65, SC 114-115
Ben Lomond, 106
Berquist Building, 20
Bicycling, MP 86, SC, 125
Big Basin Redwoods State
  Park, 106, 122
Big Sur, 42-50, *map* 46-47
Big Sur Valley, 45
Big Sur Village, 45
Big Trees Railroad, *see*
  Roaring Camp
Bird and Seal Rocks, 31, 71
Bixby Bridge, 44, 73
Boating and Fishing, MP 85,
  SC 124
Boronda History Center, 51,
  75
Bottcher's Gap, 44
Boulder Creek, 106
Butterfly Parade, 27, 68
Butterfly Trees Park, 27, 70

Cabrillo, Juan Rodriguez, 9
California's First Theater,
  22, 77
Californios, 10
Campgrounds, MP 88-90,
  SC 127-128
Cannery Row, 13, 23-26,
  69, *map* 24
Capitola, 106, *map* 107
Capitola Beach, 106
Capitola Wharf, 122
Capitular Hall, 21

Carmel, *see*
  Carmel-by-the-Sea
Carmel Art Galleries, 83-84
Carmel Bach Festival,
Carmel Beach, 38, 72
Carmel Mission, 10, 39, 72
Carmel Valley, 39-41, *map*
  40
Carmel-by-the-Sea, 35-39,
  map 36-37
Casa Abrego, 81
Casa Alvarado, 77
Casa Amesti, 81
Casa De La Torre, 82
Casa de Soto, 82
Casa del Oro, 17, 77
Casa Gutierrez (*also*
  Gutierrez Adobe), 20, 80
Casa Pacheco, 82
Casa Sanchez (*also*
  Sanchez Adobe), 20, 80
Casa Serrano, 22, 77
Casa Soberanes, 22, 77
Castle Rock State Park, 122
Castroville, 52
Centrella, The, 27
Coast Gallery, 48, 74
Cocoanut Grove Ballroom,
  100, 120
Colton Hall, 11, 21, 80
Colton, Walter, 11, 21
Constitutional Convention,
  12, 21
Cooper-Molera Adobe, 21,
  81
Cowell Beach,
Crocker Grove, 34, 72
Custom House, 16-17, 76
Custom House Plaza, 16
Cypress Point, 34, 72
Cypress Point Golf Course,
  34, 72, 88

Dana, Richard Henry, 11
Deetjen's Big Sur Inn, 48
Defense Language Institute,
  22
Del Monte Forest, 15
Del Rey Oaks, 26
DeLaveaga Park, 121
Dennis the Menace
  Playground, 23, 70
Doud House, 22, 82

Edgewater Packing
  Company, 25
El Castillo,
Elkhorn Slough, 53, 76
Esalen Institute, 49, 74
Esselen, 9

Estrada Adobe, 81

Fanshell Beach, 34, 71
Feast of Lanterns, 30
Felton, 104
Felton Covered Bridge, 104, 122
First Brick House, 20, 77
Fisherman's Wharf, 17, 70
Forest of Nisene Marks State Park, 108, 121
Forest Theater, 38
Fort Mervine, 22
Fort Ord, 26
Fremont Adobe (*also* Fremont Headquarters), 21, 81
French Consulate, 82

Garland Ranch Regional Park, 41, 73
Garrapata Beach, 44
Garrapata State Park, 73
Ghost and Witch Trees, 34, 72
Gilroy, 109
Gilroy Garlic Festival,
Golf, Game of, 135-138
Golf Courses, MP 87-88, SC 125
Gorda, 50
Gordon House, 82
Gosby House, 27
Green Gables, 27
Gutierrez Adobe, 80

Hang Gliding, 86
Harvey West Park, 121
Harvey-Baker House, 51, 75
Hearst Castle, 50, 74
Hearst, William Randolph, 50
Hecker Pass, 109
Henry Cowell Redwoods State Park, 104, 122
Henry Miller Memorial Library, 48, 74
Highlands Park, 122
History of Monterey Peninsula, 9-14
Horseback Riding, 86
Hotel Del Monte, 12, 23
Hotels, *see* Accommodations
House of Four Winds, 82
Hovden, Knute, 13
How to Get There, MP 54, SC 110
Hurricane Point, 44

Jacinto Rodriquez Adobe, *see* Rodriquez Adobe
Jade Cove, 49
Jeffers, Robinson, 39
Jolon, 49

Julia Pfeiffer Burns State Park, 49, 74

Kayaking, 86
Korean Buddhist Temple, 41, 73

La Perouse, Compte de, 10
Lake El Estero, 23
Larkin House, 11, 20, 80
Larkin, Thomas, 11
Lodge at Pebble Beach, 13, 72
Loma Prieta Earthquake, 108
Lone Cypress, 34, 72
Long Marine Laboratory, 100, 120
Lover's Point Park, 30, 70
Lucia, 49

Madariaga Adobe, 81
Marina, 27
Mayo Hayes O'Donnell Library, 22, 82
Merritt House, 22, 77
Miller Adobe, 80
Miller, Henry, 48
Mision la Exaltacion de la Santa Cruz, 101, 120
Mission Hill, 101, 120
Mission San Antonio de Padua, 49, 74
Mission San Carlos de Borromeo (*see* Carmel Mission)
Mission San Juan Bautista, 52, 76
Monterey, 16-27, *map* 18-19
Monterey Bay Aquarium, 25, 69
Monterey Canning Company, 25
Monterey Convention Center Plaza, 20
Monterey County Agricultural & Rural Life Museum, 52, 75
Monterey County Wineries, *see* Wineries
Monterey Path of History, 76-83, *map* 78-79
Monterey Peninsula, 15-98, *map*, 6, *practical information*, 54-98
Monterey Peninsula Museum of Art, 70
Monterey State Historic Park, *see* Monterey Path of History
Mopeds, 86
Moss Landing, 53
Mount Madonna Park, 109
Mystery Spot, 104, 121

Natural Bridges Beach, 100
Naval Postgraduate School, 23
Nepenthe, 48, 74
New Brighton State Beach,
Notley's Landing, 44

Octagon House, 101
Ohlone, 9
Old Monterey, 16-23
Old Monterey Jail, 80
Old Whaling Station, 20, 77

Pacific Avenue, 101
Pacific Grove, 27-30, *map* 28-29
Pacific Grove Art Center, 30, 71
Pacific Grove Natural History Museum, 30, 71
Pacific House, 17, 77
Pacific Valley, 49
Palo Colorado Canyon, 44
Partington Cove, 49
Partington Ridge, 49
Pebble Beach, 30-35, *map* 32-33
Pebble Beach Resort, 35
Pescadero Point, 34
Pfeiffer Beach, 48
Pfeiffer-Big Sur State Park, 45, 73
Pinnacles National Monument, 51, 75
Places of Interest, MP 69-76, SC 120-123
Point Joe, 31, 71
Point Lobos State Reserve, 42, 72, *map* 43
Point Pinos Reserve (*also* Point Pinos Lighthouse), 30, 71
Point Sur, 45
Point Sur Lighthouse, 34, 45
Point Sur State Historic Park, 73
Portola, Gaspar de, 10, 20
Post Hill, 48
Presidio of Monterey, 22, 82

Recreation, MP 85-87, SC 124-125
Restaurants, MP 90-98, SC 129-134
Restless Sea, 31
Roaring Camp, 104, 121
Roberts, Dr. John, 26
Rocky Creek Bridge, 44
Rocky Point, 44
Rodriguez Adobe, 20, 80
Royal Presidio Chapel, 21, 81
Rumsen, 9

Salinas, 50, 51
Salinas Old Town, 75
Salinas River State Beach, 27
San Juan Bautista, 52
San Juan Bautista State Historic Park, 52, 76
San Lorenzo Park, 121
San Lorenzo Valley, 104, *map* 105
San Simeon, 50
Sanchez Adobe, 80
Sand City, 26
Santa Cruz, 99-134, *map*, 102-103, *practical information*, 110-134
Santa Cruz Beach, 100
Santa Cruz Beaches, 125-126
Santa Cruz Boardwalk, 100, 120
Santa Cruz Harbor, 101
Santa Cruz Municipal Wharf (*also* Santa Cruz Municipal Pier), 120
Santa Cruz Museum of Natural History, 101, 121
Santa Cruz Surfing Museum, 121
Scuba Diving, 86
Seaside, 26
Seasonal Events, MP 65-69, SC 116-119
Serra, Junipero, 10, 39
17-Mile Drive (*also* Seventeen Mile Drive), 31
Sherman-Halleck Adobe, 82
Sloat, Commodore John, 11
Soledad, 51
Soquel, 106, *map* 107
Spanish Bay, 31, 71
Spirit of Monterey Wax Museum, 25, 70
Spyglass Hill, 34
Steinbeck House, 51, 75
Steinbeck Library, 51, 75
Steinbeck, John, 13, 23, 51
Stevenson House, 21, 81
Stevenson, Robert Louis, 12, 21, 34
Stoddard, Charles Warren, 12
Stokes Adobe, 82
Surfing, 125

Tennis, MP 86, SC 125
Tor House, 39, 72
Tourist Information, MP 55, SC 110
Tours, 87
Twin Lakes State Beach, 101

Underwood-Brown Adobe,
    80
University of California,
    Santa Cruz, 104, 120

Vancouver, George, 10
Vasquez Adobe, 80
Ventana Resort, 48
Ventana Wilderness, 45

Vizcaino, Sebastian, 9

Watsonville, 108
Wilder Ranch State Park,
    121
William H. Volck Museum,
    108, 122
Wineries, MP 84-85, SC,
    123-124